ABOUT THE AUTHOR

Valerie Helps was born in London and grew up in East Africa. Widely travelled, she has lived in Australia, Greece and France where she established herself as a successful travel writer and illustrator. Her short stories, poetry and children's books have been published in major newspapers and journals worldwide. She now lives in Sydney close to her family.

A CRICKET IN THE WIND
MEMORIES OF CRETE

Valerie Helps

A CRICKET IN THE WIND

MEMORIES OF CRETE

**Artwork Valerie Helps and Geoffrey Bull
Cover painting Valerie Helps**

Vanguard Press

VANGUARD PAPERBACK

© Copyright 2024
Valerie Helps

The right of Valerie Helps to be identified as the author of
this work has been asserted by her in accordance with the
Copyright, Designs and Patents Act 1988.

A CIP catalogue record for this title is
available from the British Library.

ISBN 978 1 80016 681 3

*Vanguard Press is an imprint of
Pegasus Elliot MacKenzie Publishers Ltd.*
www.pegasuspublishers.com

First Published in 2024

**Vanguard Press
Sheraton House Castle Park
Cambridge England**

Printed & Bound in Great Britain

Dedication

To my many Cretan friends, above all
to Mikalis, Marika, Yiannis and Olga for their advice and
camaraderie through the years and to Dimitris, my occasional
teacher for sharing his insight into the intricacies of the Greek
language and culture with me.

Acknowledgements

My sincere gratitude to my family, the fabulous four — Francesca, Julian, Amanda and Philippa. Without your support and enthusiasm, our sojourn on the magical Isle of Crete would not have been as much fun and as rewarding. You helped to make my dream come true.
Also my deepest thanks to my dear friends from whom I have often sought an opinion, you have listened and responded with wisdom. Your friendship is invaluable to me.

Other works by Valerie Helps

The Voyages of de Villehardouin
Cruising French Waterways
Vanguard Press (2018)
ISBN 9781784654542

A Third of a Pond
A journey around a pond
in the French countryside
Vanguard Press (2020)
ISBN 9781784656812

The Silent Towers Speak
Secrets of the Deep Mani
Vanguard Press (2021)
ISBN 9781784659776

Berrywine
A book of poems by Valerie Helps
and Laura Murray
The Magpie Press (1977)
ISBN 0 9596518 0 2

Acknowledgements by The Magpie Press in the slim volume read:
Many of Valerie's poems first appeared in the *Canberra Times*
whose permission to publish them was gratefully
acknowledged. Other poems have appeared previously in

The Saturday Club Poetry Magazine, Canberra Poetry, the *Golden
Eagle Book of Golden Verse, and the Bungendore Mirror.*

Contents

Reviews of The Silent Towers Speak

As you journey with Valerie through the Mani peninsula in Greece, all your senses are awakened. You feel the scorching heat, the exquisite light and every bump in the road, every rattle and shake of her unreliable old car. As she takes you around this lesser trodden part of the Peloponnese, you toil with her up steep hills, marvelling at her knowledge and love of the aromatic native plants; you totter down vertiginous ravines to reach little coves and the sparkling Ionian sea. You encounter goatherds with their flocks, and you visit castles and sites from antiquity.

Based in a converted Mani Tower house, Valerie explains the history of these tall, forbidding structures, dominating villages that cling to the hillsides. Previously defensive, the square towers give the Mani its unique character. You are introduced to the people; proud and wary of newcomers, yet eventually infinitely hospitable. Seasons, sunrises, sunsets, bitter winter winds and storms, local cuisine and the author's own culinary talents; all are shared in Valerie's intimate, whimsical style.

Accompanied by beautiful paintings and drawings by Valerie and partner Geoff, this book succeeded in making me feel that I know this ancient land, — and at the same time in awakening my desire to discover it for myself.

Anne Birkert
Codsall

The Silent Towers Speak - Valerie Helps' third book - is a delight to read, filled as it is with great warmth, understanding and deep appreciation of all that she encounters - and the partner with whom she encounters it - whilst resident of an ancient Maniot tower in the Deep Mani of the Peloponnese.

It is a great treat to travel with an author who has an intellectual curiosity about everything and everyone she meets as well as the artistic ability to delineate it in such a way that the reader is able to visualise that which she describes. Colours dominate in my mind - the glowing ochre of the ancient towers, dove grey shadows, 'a glimmering green and gold world', 'the ultramarine of the sea' and the 'pearly grey' cliffs. Perhaps my favourite and most empathetic moment though is the moment of being seated at the Ancient Theatre of Epidaurus anticipating the start of Sophocles' tragedy, 'Electra' ... I imagine the seats being filled with ghosts of audiences from the 400s BC.

If Covid and climate change are causing many to reconsider whether regular holiday travel is still desirable, then immersion in Valerie's book presents a suitably thorough vicarious tour of the Peloponnese, not only for its detailed descriptions of people and places but also for the delicate line drawings and paintings that are dotted throughout the book.

Joanne Gwatkin-Williams
Clyde River Retreat, South Coast NSW
Fine art print maker

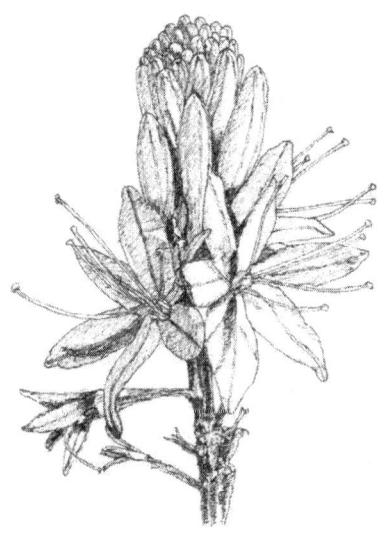

There is a land called Crete, in the midst of the wine-dark sea, a fair, rich land, begirt with water, and therein are many men, past counting, and ninety cities.

(Homer from The Odyssey)

A CRICKET IN THE WIND

Coiled spring of tiny power
calling your good luck magic
into the world
caught in the strength of
the spinning universe
where the stars
like old men with icicles
in their beards
laugh down at the earth

(Prudence Ingham)

CHAPTER ONE

"WHY CRETE?" THEY ASKED
My journey begins

"Why Crete?" they kept on asking.

"It just calls me," I said mysteriously. "I *have* to go."

They all smiled. Said how romantic. How courageous to throw away a wonderful career as orchestra manager of the Sydney Opera House resident orchestra "at your age". The phrase kept cropping up. I was fifty-five. Ready for anything — certainly a change of lifestyle.

Then they asked me what I would do when I came back, refreshed by a lengthy holiday and — they thought — dying to re-join the mad Sydney stress-scene where I seemed to spend much of my time on a physiotherapist's couch having the symptoms clicked and massaged away in my spine, only to return the next week for another, and then another session. I was always in pain and forever tired. A full night's sleep was unknown to me for in the early hours, always at around three-fifteen, my subconscious brain would propel my exhausted body into wakefulness with, quite often, the solution to one of the myriad problems that assaulted me during the daytime hours or more alarmingly, I would be reminded of some important task that I had omitted to complete or attend to so unwieldy was the workload. Fortunately it was shared by Peter, my most able assistant orchestra manager who knew the ropes after years of working in the pit. Without him I would not have lasted a week. He was so patient in dealing with my uncertainties — knowing that I had never before worked with a professional orchestra — and to be invited to join the acclaimed Sydney orchestra known as The Elizabethan Theatre Trust Orchestra was a dream come true.

*

As I write my journal on a golden gleaming day in Crete, I recall moving from Canberra to Sydney, so near the Opera House and to opera which was my great passion but also to ballet, another passion. I had a strong feeling then that maybe, just maybe, I would end up working with the opera company and be involved with those fabulous productions — and after some enjoyable years with the Sydney Youth Orchestra I was invited to fulfil my dream. I did enjoy the pace, the decisions, the buzz, the music, the voices and the supportive and marvellous musicians and most of the visiting conductors, though not all of them. Some complained endlessly about the uncomfortable air-conditioning that was always either off or far too chilly One famous conductor walked off the stage and refused to rehearse unless I did something about the air-conditioning. I immediately found the appropriate expert who raised his eyebrows in despair. It could not be altered but I persuaded him to be the person to tell our great conductor. And he was a great conductor who apologised for shouting at me; I accepted his apology with my usual charm but with the expectation of this happening again and again. And it did! It was a never-ending problem — always too hot or too cold for conductors, performers and audiences alike. I expect it will always be. Working in the opera house was a challenging and stimulating environment but after several years I suspected the stress was affecting my health, so at a family gathering on my fifty-fifth birthday, I relieved them by announcing that the dream I had been boring them with for many years was shortly to become a reality. Did they choke on their champagne? No! They cheered and hugged me. I was finally going to Crete to do something different. I intended to convert an abandoned monastery or some similar old and atmospheric building into a holiday retreat — and live in Crete forever. Mind you, I later read in the Concise Oxford Dictionary that a retreat is amongst other things:

An asylum for inebriates or lunatics or pensioners.

I hoped I didn't fit into any of those categories but I did need a rest from the whirling world; time to write and to think, maybe start sketching and painting and for several reasons only Crete would do. But I also had to earn a living. I would run holiday villas; surely *anyone* could do that?

"When are you coming back?" they asked, their eyes betraying some envy and a deal of doubt as to whether I was losing my marbles due to overwork, incredibly long hours and lack of sleep.

"I'm not!" I replied, trying to analyse my passion. It had crept in gradually through the years as I struggled with the unfamiliar cold of

Canberra winters with four children, a failing marriage and what seemed to be a bleak and hopeless future. I sought refuge in books as always, and invariably found myself drawn to the Greek section of the Woden Valley Library where my eye would scan the shelves to the Cretan section and there I would stay.

Why Crete? My reasons were deep-rooted, and I am not sure where they came from; perhaps because as a young child of three when my mother sent me to a day school in Dar es Salaam unable to cope with my unbounded energy, I was drawn to a sepia photograph — or was it a faded painting? — of the Minoan Palace of Knossos and noticed that the pillars were upside-down, thicker and broader at the top than at the bottom. I vividly recall asking the headmistress, dear, smiling, plump Mrs Zimmerman, why this was so. She did not know and had not noticed. Did my subconscious mind, ever-inquisitive some fifty years on, still need to find out *why* they were upside-down? Or perhaps it was because our civilisation began there, and the Minoan culture had always intrigued me? Or maybe it was because I was drawn to the powerful combination of mountains and sea plus the intriguing early civilisation on the island of Crete that has an abundance of all these?

*

In 1986 I visited Crete for the first time with my daughter Amanda and Mary, a Cypriot friend with whom I had been studying Greek in Canberra and the three of us drove around the island. We had only ten days, but I needed no more than half an hour to confirm that my passion was well-founded. I was instantly captivated by this craggy island with its barren, snow-covered mountain ranges and hillsides bright with wild-flowers; roads bordered with pink and white oleander interspersed with a startling yellow broom; dark gorges filled with wild cypress; a landscape decorated with soldierly stands of olives, silver in the sun; neat rows of vineyards that had produced wine since time began; fruit trees of every variety; and tiny white villages indistinguishable from the stony hillsides; this place whose surrounding seas defy description or depiction for no artist's palette has been invented that can capture the peacock green-blue-shimmering iridescence of these waters. And the Cretans — who consider themselves to be different from ordinary Greeks — I had to find out if this was so.

Most vividly I remember the lunch we shared as we explored the island. On this particular day, Mary was driving, chain-smoking as her nerves became more frayed what with being on the wrong side of the road; meeting up with donkeys ridden by little old women in black; stopping for herds of livestock; excitable dogs; jay-walking tourists behaving as if they owned the place and the mandatory chickens crossing the road. The journey was interspersed with frequent expletives as she struggled down dirt roads to investigate some sparkling beach that beckoned, or up a winding mountain forest trail to a gleaming white monastery sitting against an azure sky on the very top of a peak. Once, on a perilously steep and narrow road we met a colossal truck full of gravel whose driver refused good-naturedly to reverse, so *we* had to negotiate the entire length backwards, hoping that no one would come hurtling down the slope behind us.

It *was* nerve-wracking. Amanda sat in the back also chain-smoking, whilst I, not smoking, attempted to navigate which was an impossible task since many of the roads on the map did not even exist. Mid-afternoon and we were heading east along the north coast between Chania and Rethymnon when hunger struck. The heat was overwhelming and the sea most inviting, that wonderful indigo blue of the deep seas that turn peppermint-green in the shallows and ultramarine in the middle. Our thoughts however, were turned towards food and the road was straight and long and foodless, or so it appeared until we saw a broken-down sign pointing to a track with ταβέρνα, taverna written on it in squiggly letters. The narrow path was rough and overgrown but we followed it down towards the sea thinking we would have to turn back as it led nowhere, but on turning a corner, we came across a dilapidated two-storey stone villa with shuttered windows sitting in a farmyard. It was none too inviting; goats, hens, ducks and dirt surrounded the building; the guard dog was in keeping with the place, shaggy and unkempt. But friendly. The air was hot and rank with the stench of old chicken and animal droppings and piles of rotting vegetables oozing in a corner; rusty petrol cans, a broken wheelbarrow, old bottles and tins, tyres and broken sacks all enclosed by a leaning fence and a few drooping flowers completed the scene. Not exactly what we had in mind. This surely could not be *the taverna*.

Along one side of the small property was an orchard of gnarled and neglected fruit trees; oranges, apricots, figs and broad-leaved loquats and as we parked in the drive I noticed large ripe lemons growing on the trees. It had once been a beautiful place. The terrace was shaded by a disintegrating wooden pergola covered with grapevines above a few rickety tables and chairs, bleached by the sun. Just visible through several old and ragged tamarisks was the sea where sharp rocks jutted out into the deep, waves gently breaking on a tiny bay. There was no one about so we decided to have a swim and cool off before driving farther to look for lunch and were just about to change when a man hailed us from the house. He was rotund and somewhat dishevelled with untidy hair and it looked as if we had disturbed his siesta. Did we want something? Mary's Greek was better than mine and she discovered that indeed we had woken him from his siesta; δεν πειράζει, den pirazi he replied, it does not matter and that indeed it was a taverna and yes, we could have lunch. We immediately ordered *marithes,* whitebait with chips and a Greek or village salad which luckily I knew in Greek as *horiatiki saláta* — and went for a swim in the blessed coolth of the peppermint shallows as the sea washed away the dust of the day. We dived and came up with dolphin-sleek hair feeling the salt on our skins.

"What a find!" we called to one another. "What a find!"

As we dried ourselves, tingling and refreshed from the shining waters I watched a small girl with gleaming black curls drag a table and chairs beneath one of the trees by the water's edge, she kicked at the chickens as they grumbled around her bare feet watched by a cautious cat, sitting safely under a hibiscus. Well out of the way. Sometime later, the man came out laden with dishes followed by a dumpy woman in an apron and the child carrying an armful of plates, all smiling broadly as they set the table with much noise and discussion then called us to the feast, and a feast it was. Hot, brown farm bread coarse and springy, cut into big chunks; a Greek salad the size of a mountain topped with huge slabs of feta cheese doused with glaucous delicious virgin olive oil of that greenish tinge found only when it comes straight from the trees, liberally sprinkled with fresh oregano; a bowl of τζατζίκι, tzatziki, made with yoghurt, grated cucumber, dill and reeking of garlic; delicious Cretan chips cut through the middle and fried to perfection and the fish. Oh the fish! A mountain of small fish piled high on an outsize plate, crisply fried and browned with the aromatic mixture of herbs and lemon juice filling the air and our nostrils as we leaned forward breathing in the delicious aromas. Had we died and gone to heaven?

We stood up and applauded with one voice, "πολύ καλά! poli kala!" very good! as we raised our glasses to the smiling man and his wife who were chastising the child who was again kicking the chickens. We squeezed the pale lemons still warm from the trees on the tiny fish and began to eat, we were all seriously hungry and hardly knew where to begin. A satisfied silence reigned as we finished the meal washed down with cold glasses of sweet water; further comment was unnecessary there were no words to express our contentment. Crete was filled with magic, the meal was superb, the chef was an artist.

A long time later with the empty plates piled high with remains which were feeding three cats that had appeared out of the shadows, the man asked us if we wanted Greek coffee. Indeed we did. He brought three small white cups with three more glasses of ice-cold water as the little girl danced nearby, twisting and turning, laughing, her dark curls flying loose and glistening. A child's laughter in the sea air. An enchanting free child. Uninhibited.

We sat back on our rickety chairs, replete and utterly content and talked idly of this and that, how nice it would be to own a place like this and 'do it up' and run it. Just the three of us. But we would not want to change it too much we all agreed it would remain much the same, just the odd nail here and there and a general clean-up.

Then I said, "But they wouldn't want to sell, they're blissfully happy here aren't they?" And then,

"What if some ghastly tourists came to invade our little bit of heaven, we would have to be polite and serve them. How would we manage that?"

Amanda's tawny lion eyes met mine and narrowed slightly. Mary's black almond eyes met mine, screwed up as the smoke from yet another cigarette clouded her vision. Neither of them said a word. We thought for a few moments, sipping our thick, sweet coffee as the wind rustled through the feathery needles of the tamarisks to the soft cooing of the doves. No. Perhaps it was not such a good idea after all. We would leave it as it was — we had met a memorable chef and enjoyed a memorable lunch in a memorable taverna with its feet in the ocean. This was an enchanted place where the doves nested on a rock far out in the shallows and the cicadas told us persistently that it was summer.

I remember every detail as if it were yesterday; sitting in our costumes with salt-stiff hair and the sun on our backs filtering through the tamarisks, the sea beyond and all of Crete beckoning and it confirmed what I had known all along — that Crete was right for me. I knew it from within the deep core of my being. I also knew my family would applaud and be as supportive as possible as they are all four of them born with a sense of adventure. What I did not know at that time however, was that my son and his wife and one of my daughters had become jaded with city life and that they would drop everything and come along too!

*

Following our new and delicious gourmet experience I had to find out exactly what we had been eating. The fish was known in Greek as *marithes*, whitebait in English and I knew that young fish were known as 'fry' – I figured that when I was running my holiday villas at least I would be able to describe this most desirable dish with an aplomb that would imply I had always known what *marithes* were. I had only come across them once before during my childhood in Tanganyika, with my ayah Binti Isa with her tightly plaited hair and her small round Bantu face with its many cicatrices. She would share her whitebait with me; the species from the Indian Ocean were larger and very crunchy and we ate them whole which initially I found a bit distasteful but she would devour them at a rate of knots with a mouth almost bare of front teeth and when she giggled — which she often did — her gums were more visible than her teeth. What happened to her teeth I used to ask at which she would chuckle further, smooth down her coloured clothing, always bright on her tiny frame — lean forward to touch my face, then throw her neat head backwards and smack her hands on her thighs with delight. I really loved her — this tiny woman — my childhood ayah and I do believe she loved me. My name in Swahili is '*Velwe*'.

*

Speaking of names — 'Valerie' written in Greek is '*Βαλερί*' which looks a bit like 'Balepi' and that's what my family calls me. I love it. However, the name 'Valérie' with an accent is old and of Latin and French origin, it means 'healthy and strong.' That's encouraging!

*

And so it was that my eldest daughter Francesca, known as 'Chanky' her childhood nickname that is still installed in my brain, my son Julian and his new French wife Nathalie and I flew out of rainy Sydney to Crete and adventure. I gave my beloved Burmese cat D'Artagnan to my good friend Bunty and left behind my two younger daughters in floods of tears and yes, I felt guilty, but not guilty enough to turn back; after all, they had their partners and their own lives and Crete had been calling for too long. I was on my way!

Two days in hot, throbbing Athens with the marvel of the Acropolis at dawn and a memorable lunch high on the hill beneath vines heavy with grapes in a taverna called — believe it or not *Allo!* '*Allo!* So inappropriate for it was very Greek, not French at all. We began with the Greek toast before sipping our ice-cool wine, clinking our glasses with a combined *"Stin yia mas!"* To you/our health! as we gorged on fresh Greek salads and delectable *spanakopitas,* cheese and spinach pies while absorbing the unsurpassable scene spread out below us and rising up behind us into the bluest of blue skies — the clean pure lines of the Parthenon.

We endured a rough overnight ferry to Crete with passengers in sleeping bags lining the deck and sprawled over all the couches and easy chairs in the vast saloon that was equipped, or rather blighted might be the more appropriate word, with television sets in each of the four corners, broadcasting on different channels with the volume turned to full decibels. And *everyone* smoked. Our four-berth cabin was cramped and well below the waterline, it seemed to be next door to the engine — noisy and somewhat claustrophobic to say the least. After a most excellent meal in the well-appointed saloon, we retired — we thought — to our tiny quarters. Nathalie was the first to visit the 'heads', the marine lavatory and as she pulled the chain, a deafening and violent jet of seawater boiled into the pan virtually ejecting her off the seat and at the very same moment, the boat's engines started up accompanied by a thunderous roar that gave us all a colossal fright. She came hurtling out as though she had been shot from a canon, knickers and slacks around her ankles, blue eyes wide with shock and raced out of the cabin into the corridor. Serious pacifying, including a walk around the deck was needed before she regained her composure. The episode has had us in fits of laughter ever since.

Sleep evaded us. The cabin was so cramped, we were all over-tired and excited when finally Francesca, who had become bored with watching Julian's socks which, for some reason known only to himself, were pegged over her bunk and swayed to and fro just above her nose, decided that she and Nathalie, both feeling somewhat seasick, would retire to the saloon and spend the rest of the short night away from the stuffy cabin.

Next morning, fortified by double Greek coffees we cruised into the port of Heraklion at dawn with the sun on the White Mountains rising sheer behind the ugly concrete town. To arrive by sea is the only way to approach the island of Crete with the Venetian fortress in the foreground glowing pink in the early morning light. I was thrilled beyond words as we leaned over the deck in the cold air as the surrounding mountains beckoned us to explore. And explore we did, clocking up a thousand kilometres in an expensive hire car booked in Sydney; we found out later that one can get them cheaper locally. Crete, although the largest of the Greek islands is quite small, being 260 kilometres long and 60 kilometres wide the massive central spine of mountains rising twelve hundred metres makes much of the island impassable by road.

In the far west, we stayed in Chania with its delightful Venetian port and lighthouse; the Venetians ruled Crete for four hundred years and left their mark throughout the island. With a sky full of wheeling swallows, we joined the locals as they took their evening *volta,* stroll, along the waterfront. We slept in dreadful narrow beds in a Venetian house with a winding, creaking wooden staircase, wooden shutters and very high ceilings. The typical Greek lavatory was a lean-to on a flat roof where due to the narrow pipes the *used* loo paper had to be dispensed in a plastic container beside the seat. A visit to be avoided by later afternoon in summer believe me!

*

My aim was to purchase and convert a secluded hilltop monastery, miles away from all signs of habitation and turn it into a sanctuary for artists, writers and musicians — a creative place to enable guests to escape the whirling world and speak my kind of language. However, my ever-practical son pointed out that those creative people seldom had any money.

"Interesting though they may be," he added, not wanting to scoff at my dreams while stroking my shoulders as he made his valid point.

"And if we are miles away from the main road how are we going to attract passers-by? Until we get our publicity up and going we will need passing customers won't we?"

I could see the logic but I was not really interested in making money, I just wanted a rewarding life meeting people with whom I have an affinity and I was prepared to work hard to achieve it. Sadly, monasteries are not for sale said the gentle-eyed monk whom we disturbed from his siesta at the Monastery of Panagia Chrysoskalitissa, on the outer tip of the southwest coast at the end of a diabolical dirt road. The seventeenth-century monastery sleeps in the afternoon sun while hundreds of metres far below, the waves crash into a deep cove and a dark-robed nun smiles nervously from within her shadowy cell. Archways lead nowhere but to a flowering cactus, sleeping lizards and wildflowers on ancient walls. The original nunnery was built in the tenth century and in the last century there were two hundred inhabitants and now there are only two, a monk and a nun — plus the tourists. Where have they all gone? Later research tells me that in nineteen hundred, the monastery was dissolved along with other monasteries in Crete and reinstated as a female nunnery forty years later.

The island of Elafonisi five kilometres further south on an even worse road spread out before us and the clear waters invited us for a swim. In good weather the island can be reached by walking through the shimmering shallows to the sandy beach. The intriguing pink tinge in the sand is due to the many thousands of crushed seashells. The dunes were warm, but the sea was cold and the wind brisk, whipping the fine sand into our eyes so we did not stay long. Similar to some of the beaches further north there were patches of black tar from passing ships which once on our clothes was impossible to eradicate.

Palaiochora looked inviting from the high mountain road, but the approach was through a stinking rubbish dump and in the night, the Libyan sirocco whistled violently around like some crazed demon, rattling doors and shutters and chasing our balcony chairs to and fro making sleep almost impossible. We left early with the smell of dust in our nostrils and headed north through craggy mountain ranges then south again to Frangokastello on the coast, through Vrysses, cool and green, shaded by colossal plane trees under which we had a memorable picnic to the sound of rushing water.

Frangokastello — apricot in colour with crenellated turrets and reputedly haunted though we failed to see the ghostly horsemen at dawn. It looks like a complete castle from the outside but is only a shell, redolent with the acrid smell of urine and thick with weeds. Fortunately the hotel-cum-taverna we found on the seafront was delightful and we stayed two days, drinking good Cretan wine, eating our fill of Greek salads and local cheeses and swimming in the clearest waters, our minds floating about on the cool evening breezes. Relaxed. Protected by the mountains all around us. Francesca on the other hand, spent most of her time evading the amiable and amorous hotel owner who was much taken by her blonde beauty.

We called into the tiny port of Chora Sfakion and watched Arab fishermen tending their nets on a fishing boat, listening to the plaintive music of their culture. They seemed unaware of us as they worked, happy and contented with their lot.

Rethymnon — with its massive Venetian fortress, reputedly the largest ever built and its long beach lined with miles of bright awnings sheltering the fragile skins of northern visitors; an overpowering waft of suntan oil and bright-eyed waiters, all very good-looking encouraged one politely to stop for a drink or a meal. This was the first time we had been approached by touts and we did not like it. We investigated the old part through winding back streets with ornate doors and Turkish balconies that seemed to almost touch one another across streets so narrow we had to reverse out. Once out of the tourist belt, we enjoyed a truly Greek meal of *gigantes,* giant beans steeped in tomato and swimming in delicious olive oil with spicy *keftedes*, meatballs, and Cretan chips washed down with sharp *retsina*, that resinated white wine to which we were fast becoming addicted; so refreshing on a hot day.

*

The mountain roads offered spectacular views and wound through fields of scarlet poppies and a profusion of wildflowers on the lower slopes. Chestnut, oak, pine and cypress — the latter once covered the island — grew thickly in the ravines while the hillsides were terraced to great heights with stands of olives and lower down with vineyards. On the coastal plains, acres of vegetables, many undercover and a blot on the beautiful landscape, but Crete produces the earliest vegetables, fruit and flowers in Europe and the export market is healthy indeed. We stopped at many beaches, tamarisk-shaded with unbelievably clear waters; stretched our legs in tiny mountain hamlets watched mostly by old Cretans with fine features and light eyes; shepherds with flocks of sheep and goats often blocked our way and mules laden high with produce or bales of yellow hay ridden by little old women with black stockings, were a common sight. All raised their hands with a cheery καλημέρα, kalimera good-day. Cretans are a friendly lot.

One early morning we wandered around a deserted Knossos, Palace of the Minoans, dreaming beneath the dark pines. Atmospheric. For all the criticism levelled at Arthur Evans' rapid reconstruction, unless one has studied Minoan history and architecture the other Minoan palaces on the island mean little if one has not first visited today's Knossos; the remains of these are just 'a pile of bricks and mortar' to an ignoramus like me. I told myself I would like to get some kind of work — any kind — at Knossos and learn more about this marvellous lost civilisation.

*

'Plant the seed and the seed will grow' has always been my philosophy. I have planted the seed and I will work there I feel certain. θα δούμε, tha thoume —we will see, the Greeks so often wisely say as they finger their κομπολόγια, komboloiya, worry beads.

*

I pondered over every location we visited, could I live there? And the answer was always no, for the dream in my mind's eye was truly clear. I *knew* that waiting for me somewhere in Crete was a steeply terraced hillside of stark white villas, each standing on top of the other between the dark shapes of citrus trees and across a blue bay —

a range of barren and jagged mountains. I could see the villas and I thought they were on that peninsula in north-western Crete, but when we drove there we couldn't find them! I must have been mistaken about the exact position but I knew they were there — somewhere. Waiting for me perhaps? How long would we continue driving around the island in search of this dream? As long as it takes, I told myself. Luckily my family understood and there was no hurry.

CHAPTER TWO

SANTORINI
Is this the lost continent of Atlantis?

Tired of driving we took a ferry to the volcanic island of Santorini. As we docked at Athinio, a tiny port almost nudged into the sea by vertical red cliffs we were immediately besieged by hordes of smiling, beguiling touts holding placards advertising scooter and car hire; minibus and taxi services; restaurants and night-clubs; island tours; δωμάτιο για ενοικίαση, thomatio yia enikiasi, rooms for rent and hotels.

"Very special villa. Only five hundred metres from middle of town. Ella! Ella!" Come, come! Invited the taxi drivers en masse. "Come to look!"

"Oh yes — five-hundred metres? More like five-thousand metres!" we mocked.

One of them raised his eyebrows and replied laughingly, "Ochi!" No, that would be off the end of the island!

Unable to make any sensible decisions regarding anything at all in the ensuing chaos we made our choice, we hoped, and with the cynicism of the well-travelled opted for the bus, stowed our bags into its depths and climbed aboard. I was about to sit down when I had the alarming and very real sensation of our bus *moving backwards* — and I knew we were not far from the edge of the quay and the depth of the caldera of Santorini where our bus would disappear forever, so I shouted to the others and leapt out and began to scrabble like a mad woman in the hold, for our bags. Francesca climbed out after me in astonishment and yelled,

"Mum! What the hell are you doing?" I tried to explain breathlessly that our bus was moving backwards into the sea and I wanted to rescue our baggage.

"Where are the others? Why are they still on the bus for god's sake?" I had visions of them going down in the bus to the deep blue depth of the harbour.

"Mum," my daughter said in her patient voice that barely conceals her irritation with her mother on occasions. "*We* are not moving. It's the *other bus* alongside that is going forward hence the illusion of us going backwards."

And she was right of course! I felt such an idiot as I clambered back followed by what seemed like hundreds of pairs of eyes filled with utter astonishment. We still laugh at this.

Our bus groaned and whined up the tortuous road along the edge of the steep escarpment negotiating unbelievably tight hairpin bends carved out of the perpendicular rock face. Twice we stopped — and I wondered fleetingly how often the brakes were checked — once to allow another bus to reverse to get around a tight corner and again when a car had parked badly and its driver was taking photos of the port, now in miniature far down below. Traffic had come to a standstill, but nobody seemed to mind and following some good-natured shouting and waving of hands he moved on and we parted company, all smiles and sweat. It was *hot!*

Once in the gleaming white town of Thera we found rooms for rent and did what everyone does on Santorini; we hired scooters and toured the island though I had not ridden even a bicycle for some thirty-five years. Away we went, wind in our hair and freedom in our wheels and speaking for myself with wobbly knees and my heart in my mouth but it was glorious and our shrieks and laughter drew attention from all the passers-by. I came off in a ditch on the first day and was persuaded to settle my nerves by having a puff on someone's cigarette — I don't smoke and it only made me feel sick and caused a great deal of merriment. What I needed was a stiff gin and tonic! I got on again with legs more unsteady than ever and a thumping heart but was determined not to be a killjoy on this exciting adventure. It was the *only* way to see the island. We explored the gleaming white villages and blue-domed churches — not all of them: there are allegedly fifty blue-domed churches on Santorini — swam off black volcanic beaches into icy seas and ate *gyros;* delicious chunks of sliced meat, tomatoes and yoghurt and fried onions wrapped in unleavened bread while watching the famous sunset over the bay a thousand feet below. Provided one can ignore the trendy, tourist atmosphere of Santorini it is a stunning place to visit — preferably out of season as we were, though the tiny town of Thera was thick with the loud voices of mostly American women from the latest tourist boat, buying up everything they could find at inflated prices much to the obvious amusement of the locals.

We had a highly entertaining bus trip both to and from the extraordinary excavations at Akrotiri that lie at the bottom of a steep escarpment at the southern tip of the island. We caught a local bus in the square in Thera that rapidly filled up from full to overflowing as more and more passengers climbed in; we were jammed in like proverbial sardines and just as smelly from where I was sitting. The heat was searing and the road rough and tortuously twisting and winding and we were thrown against one another time and time again — apologies — mainly in German and the stale stench of hairy underarms. At one stop a village woman wanted to dismount, and the retrieval of her mop and plastic bucket from beneath people's legs was a major event accompanied by cheers of good humour and encouragement as passengers got off the bus to make room for her. She stumbled off and all the passengers climbed back in again and the driver revved the engine, took his foot off the accelerator and shouted something unintelligible out of the window to the woman who was standing in the middle of the road waving her mop at him.
She had forgotten something. "Oh no!" we groaned. Everybody off as she climbed in again with downcast eyes and scrambled beneath our legs until she found her bag of shopping. More cheers and we finally got underway.

Once at the site Francesca and Nathalie amused themselves while Julian and I explored the ancient settlement that has lain sleeping for over two thousand years. Currently under excavation, the town has produced gorgeous frescoes, pottery contemporary with that of Crete, jewellery, furnishings, and even the remains of food have been found in this Minoan Pompeii with its beautifully preserved buildings lying beneath the thick blanket of volcanic lava and pumice. The excavation is fully under cover and to walk through the streets of the town is strangely eerie; there is an unaccountable silence and people tend to whisper as one enters a world devoid of colour but for the pinky-beige of the volcanic dust that covers everything. Buildings, walls, steps, giant *pithoi* earthenware jars merge and glow in a muted monotone which is quite disorientating after the blazing sun and deep blue of the sea outside. Julian and I had the distinct impression of activity around us of small people still at work, potters, stonemasons, and builders. It was a productive place — creative too. And they were still there; we could *feel* them around us and they did seem to be slighter in size than today's humans. Interestingly, no skeletons of humans or animals except that of a pig have been found which implies the inhabitants had sufficient warning to allow them to collect their animals, valuables including their tools, before the mass migration.

Research suggests a massive earthquake well before the volcanic eruption most likely caused the inhabitants to flee before the final disaster destroyed their civilisation. Seeds that were left in the ruins of the houses following the earthquake had begun to germinate before the first ash from the eruption fell; so where did they go? To Crete — the centre of Minoan civilisation that lies ninety-five kilometres to the south — or did they all perish at sea? The force of the eruption blew out the centre of the island leaving a vast caldera where ferries and sleek liners now lie at anchor in the deep, dark waters. The eruption was followed by a *tsunami,* which it is claimed also destroyed the Minoan palaces in Crete. Many believe the island was the original lost continent of Atlantis, the legendary city that mysteriously disappeared into the sea. Plato in his dialogues between two learned men, Timaeus and Critias, tells of a great island *west* of Spain where:

"There came terrible earthquakes and floods, and in the course of a day and a night full of horrors the entire island of Atlantis vanished beneath the waves".

Santorini or Thera, is *east* of Spain not west, and it is unlikely that Plato would have made a mistake, however several learned men have placed Ancient Thera, or Fira or Santorini as being the most likely site of mythical Atlantis and it teases the imagination to fantasise. Santorini has become the more commonly used name, derived from the island's patron saint, Irene. The story makes fascinating reading and having wandered through the silent streets I could be persuaded to believe in almost anything.

We planned to be first on the return bus to secure good seats but it was already too late and I, undoubtedly due to my increasing years, was the only one of us to get a seat; well, I sat gingerly on a plank of wood suspended between the two back seats tightly squeezed between two cheerful Canadians. The other three stood in front of me and leaned against two of the seats; there were no straps to hang on to and the bus lurched and swayed in its usual fashion as it groaned up the steep incline, stopping frequently to let more and more passengers on. Each time it lurched, all those standing fell against the person beside them only to be thrown the other way a second later as we wound up the tortuous road to Thera. As we neared the town my family with one accord burst into hysterical giggles that rapidly became raucous laughter, their eyes filling with tears, seemingly quite unable to control themselves. It was so contagious that those around them began to laugh until the entire back section of the bus was seized with a sort of infectious hysteria, probably brought on not only by whatever it was that triggered their mirth, and I was dying to find out, but also by the heat and discomfort — and possibly real fear! I mean how often do they check the brakes on Greek buses I asked myself yet again? I was longing to join in the joke but was trapped behind the most colossal bottom of an overweight and extremely sweaty woman. As soon as we climbed off, I tried to discover what had amused them so much but they were still laughing uncontrollably, holding their stomachs and bending over with exhaustion. Finally I discovered the reason for their merriment: Francesca, who was standing behind Julian, had been hanging on to what she thought was his belt but wondered why she got so little support from this and it wasn't until a particularly violent lurch caused her to fall away from him, that she realised she had been hanging onto her *own* bum bag belt! And Nathalie had a good grip on what she thought was the top of the seat in front of her — a sort of soft fabric substance — when the same lurch dislodged her from her hold and the 'fabric' came away in her hand. It turned out to be a handful of hair belonging to the Greek woman in front who appeared

43

not to notice. Nathalie still had the hair in her hand when she got off the bus. Ah, the joys of public transport in Greece!

*

High winds marooned us on the island for a week until a large ferryboat, the only ship big enough to tackle the turbulent Sea of Crete, took us off at midnight. It was heading for Agios Nikolaos. We had planned to return to Heraklion and hire yet another car to continue our exploration, and interestingly, this was not a priority on our visiting list due to its reputation of being too touristy for words with mostly 'lager louts' in the summer from Britain! But Fate takes a hand when we least expect it.

So — as luck would have it — we disembarked at dawn at the small port of Agios Nikolaos overlooking the Bay of Mirabello, sheltered by surrounding mountains. It was cool and grey yet as we climbed the steep tree-lined streets reading our *Let's Go Greece* travel guide in search of somewhere to stay, we all experienced the same feeling of well-being. We really liked this small and inviting port, its deep lake and the geese and ducks. Everything about it in fact. In our temporary rent rooms I did a little reading in a more informative paperback and discovered that this port is as old as the hills, positively reeking with history and this region was once an important prehistoric settlement on Crete. I loved the feeling that I was standing where others have stood — how many centuries ago? The answer to that question is that Crete was the centre of the Minoans, the first advanced European civilization on the island from around 3000BC to 1100BC, and that will lead to resolving my childhood query at school in Dar es Salaam which was to find out why the pillars at the Minoan Palace of Knosssos appeared to be upside-down, broader at the top than at the base. I was excited at the prospect. The palace was so close and I was almost certain we would settle in this area. I also had a strong feeling that I would one day somehow become involved with and become familiar with the lives of the Minoans. My fascination was intense and backed by that inner knowledge that I have always been unable to explain. The history and mythology of the palace were familiar to me, the stories of Icarus and Daedalus, the Labyrinth and the terrifying Minotaur. I couldn't wait to stand on the site and look across the valleys to the hills and *feel* the centuries beneath my feet; knowing that aeons ago someone had stood there gazing at the same view perhaps with the same dreams as I had. Soon I would not just be looking at books, I would have arrived. What made it even more rewarding was that I would be sharing this with members of my family — how could one be so lucky I kept asking myself? There must be some Greek god somewhere who is smiling upon us all.

*

When we arrived the season was just beginning and the town was throbbing with activity. Spring-cleaning was in progress, the pavements littered with ladders, tins of paint, upturned tables and chairs, replacement awnings and blinds; cats observing the unusual bustle from the safety of a sunny sill; gypsy trucks plied up and down laden with pot plants and plastic furniture with loudspeakers turned up to deafening decibels; tavernas blared out familiar bouzouki sounds; hoses cleaned the accumulated sirocco dust from Libya off the buildings. The place was alive after the quiet days of winter. Agios Nikolaos lies on the western side of the Bay of Mirabello, well sheltered from storms and winds that according to legend, made it a favourite bolthole for the pirate Barbarolli in the fifteenth century. The tree-lined town is built on hills and sits with its feet in what was once considered by the locals to be a bottomless lake. Lake Voulismeni *does* have a bottom and it is sixty-four metres deep with red perpendicular cliffs bordering one side. Brightly painted *caiques*, fishing boats, line its curves and tavernas front onto the lake where ducks waddle between the tables competing with the cats.

We soon discovered Asteria, a typical Greek καφενεῖον, café, with rickety chairs and tables right on the harbour's edge against the tour boats that fortunately had not yet begun their frantic to-ing and fro-ing to the island of Spinalonga, lying off the little fishing port of Elounda. In my careful Greek, I ordered καφέ φραπέ, iced coffee for four; the French word *frappé* describes an iced drink and in Crete that means a frothy, foamy Nescafe shaken with ice cubes and water. We sat on our spindly chairs grinning inanely at one another, the sun warm on our backs. Once again, we agreed that we liked this little port though we had vowed to avoid it; it was May and not a lout of any nationality was to be seen, and it was certainly the prettiest place we had visited, though we had liked Chania. We would stay for a while. Definitely.

CHAPTER THREE

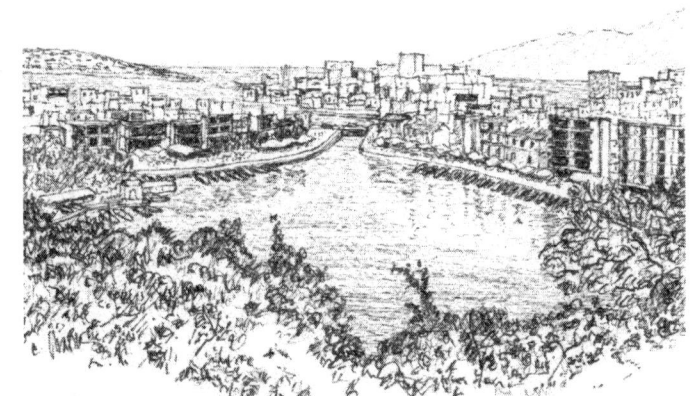

WE DISCOVER VILLA OLGA
Georgina and the Green House

The four of us were staying temporarily at the Green House which wasn't green at all but did have dark green shutters and doors. It sat just up the hill from the port past the tiny church. It was owned by Georgina, a weary yet sharp-eyed Cretan woman in her mid-fifties who had established an amazing garden up two flights of stairs, in a courtyard around which small rooms opened. Plants, shrubs and fruit trees grew in wild profusion on this upper-level garden whose occupants included a tortoise, a cat and a scruffy poodle named Mannix. Georgina only fed the cat, she told us in her fractured English — the dog scrounged around the streets for food and was heartily cuffed if he had not returned to spend the night with her on the hammock which was strung between a pillar and a tree, for Georgina like most Greeks in tourist-popular centres, vacated and rented out her quarters for the season; slept on a hammock in the tiny garden and lived in her cramped kitchen. Her clothes hung in the narrow space she called her laundry — and on any spare hook she could find — and she spent her entire day endlessly washing white sheets and pillowcases which, when drying, festooned the flat roofs that overlooked the Green House on either side. She also owned a shop below that sold natural fertilisers, garden things and herbal medicines. Georgina would catch forty winks whenever possible in her hammock, her wrinkled skirt riding up to show the bare flesh above the top of her knee-length stockings and her yellow knitted cardigan wrapped around her for it can be quite cool in May. The telephone for the 'rooms for rent', was connected to a deafening klaxon so she could hear it when downstairs in the shop, but when it woke her from her catnap her eyes held a look of intense anxiety as she was briefly disorientated. This woman was in a state of chronic exhaustion and the season had not begun.

We were not particularly comfortable in our two rooms — no, that's wrong — start again. We were not at *all* comfortable in our two rooms; the mattresses appeared to be stuffed with concrete and the pillows with a similar unyielding substance and the primitive bathroom consisted of a lavatory-cum-shower which when on sprayed both the loo, the container for the used loo paper, the basin and the entire floor including one's towel or any clothes, finally running out into the garden which on reflection, was a good utilisation of water. There were nine bedrooms so the queue in the morning was interesting. We had been there three days before I discovered another tiny lavatory at the back of the so-called laundry, where Georgina had her washing machine. That did help and the other guests — mainly Germans staying overnight en route elsewhere — didn't know about it.

Food was not permitted in the rooms and we certainly could not afford to have all our meals in tavernas — cheap though they were — so this necessitated secreting items of food into the rooms and trusting she would not smell the delicious aroma of cheese pies; the brewing of furtive cups of coffee on our tiny primus and switching it off quickly and shoving it under the bed when Georgina passed by – and she was always everywhere– became increasingly difficult so we decided to investigate self-contained apartments since we intended to explore this part of Crete which so far, we liked better than any other we had seen.

Georgina was extremely helpful. She knew someone who had an apartment, two in fact, and he was just down the road. A telephone call and we met the man at midday who turned out to be the same good-looking Cretan from whom we had hired a car earlier on. The upper floor apartment was newly completed. Pristine — but it was rented for six weeks. There was another apartment he said brightly so off we go, down to the ground floor — no — to *below* the ground floor. This was incomplete with tiny rooms and small windows higher than anyone's eye level. Not natural light at all — a dungeon no less and it was surprisingly overpriced. We thanked him politely and informed Georgina on our return. She pursed her lips and made another call.

This time we were to go 'very close' to meet a woman who had an apartment. We would like this one she said rolling her black eyes; it was πολύ μεγάλο, poli megalo, very big. It sounded fine. We followed her instructions, got lost in the winding and very hilly streets for which there were no visible road names and finally, twenty minutes later when my feet were about to give up, an elderly woman in black hailed us. She had a plastic bag full of cleaning materials which we felt to be somewhat inauspicious. She led the way past several blocks of unfinished concrete shells; shabby shops and shabbier tavernas, rubbish dumps and broken cars until the road became a weed-infested dirt track that turned inland. More decrepit buildings. It was becoming increasingly apparent that we were decidedly on the wrong side of town. Then she struck out across a field of dried grass and sharp thistles along a narrow path towards a derelict building. I called out weakly to my lagging family.

"Well we're not living there!" Aware of a slight hysteria in my tone as we all began to giggle, trying to suffocate our mirth for fear of offending her; there was a certain dignity about our leader that could not be questioned. We followed obediently as she veered away from the building into an olive grove; we were now right out of town. We considered asking her to stop but were by now intrigued to find out exactly where she was taking us. We were all keen to live in the country rather than in the town — but where was the approach road? Eventually we arrived at a large double-storied Cretan building still in the throes of completion — aren't they all? As we climbed the outer stairs we looked down onto a group of shacks attached to the main structure. In the central yard was a Rastafarian with wild locks and layers of bright clothing in a passionate clinch with a young girl who could have been underage, while another man looked on with amusement. All somewhat seedy-looking and not quite the sort of neighbours we envisaged — in fact we were determined not to have any neighbours at all. Pop music blared out to complete the atmosphere of decadence. We took one look at the unfinished apartments which might have been quite suitable, thanked our now distinctly unfriendly potential landlady and headed back the way we came — cross-country with sandals full of dust. Giggling uncontrollably. This was what we wanted to experience; another culture, another way of life and perhaps a little disturbingly, a portent of things to come regarding accommodation?

On returning to the Green House Georgina's lips pursed even tighter. Bootlacey around the mouth. Was the apartment really so unsuitable? And so far away? With no road? "*Poh poh!*" Meanwhile she would make another telephone call, but we protested and said we were going by car to look further out of town as her ideas had drawn a blank.

"Shall we search again tomorrow?" I suggested weakly. Silent approval from the family as we collapsed outside Asteria by the bottomless lake and ordered refreshments as our feet gradually recovered.

*

Driving north along the road that winds along the steep hillside we passed one luxury hotel after another, gleaming white with simple Cretan lines and luxuriant gardens already bursting with flowers, attractive in their own way but one could imagine the awful crowds during summer. This coastline was almost unheard of before the two BBC television series *Who pays the Ferryman* and *The Lotus Eaters*, both of which I saw and drooled over when living in Australia, brought Agios Nikolaos and Elounda to the attention of the British public. A major hotel was built, then another and mass tourism with all its horrors began as the little harbour town of Agios Nikolaos — population 8,500 — stretched to 50,000 beds every summer. It was this reputation that had made me decide to avoid this town. I wanted to find small, quality holiday villas in an isolated fishing village somewhere to attract visitors in search of tranquillity and a purely Cretan way of life *but* Julian reminded me yet again, that we had to make a living from tourism so initially at least we had to be on or near a main road to attract passers-by. Later, when we became known we could retire to a quieter more desirable location to carry out my dream. He was right of course.

*

It was the garden that captivated us first of all. We were about seven kilometres out of Agios Nikolaos heading for Elounda when we saw it — the wrought iron gate, a cluster of white villas clambering up one on top of another along the terraced hillside, the intense scarlet of geraniums and hibiscus, magenta and purple bougainvillaea growing in giant-sized ceramic pots and beneath laden fruit trees, gleaming pieces of marble scattered around the terraces. A rusty sign by the gate on the road said 'Villa Olga. Furnished Apartments'. And a phone number. We would look around Elounda and the coast farther north, swim then call in on the way back.

However, 'the best-laid plans of mice and men'… on reaching the charming port of Elounda we decided it was too hot to look for apartments and the sea too inviting so we bought local cheese, tomatoes, cucumbers, olives and a two-litre bottle of Cretan red in a small shop, followed our noses to the bakery down a narrow lane and bought a loaf of blisteringly hot bread. A short drive down a path led us to shady tamarisks where we spent the rest of the day lying around, eating and swimming in crystal waters.

We almost did not stop at Villa Olga for the idea of a late siesta before supper was uppermost in our minds even though we had done nothing all day. Living there did that to one. Maybe it was the wine — or the sun or the sighing of the wind in the tamarisk trees — or the heat — or the cicadas. Who knew or cared for that matter? Fortunately, the villas were on the same side of the road as we were so not too much energy was required to stop the car and investigate. The wrought-iron gate was difficult to open; my mind noted this as something we would have to fix as soon as we lived there and I knew then, that we would. We had found my dream place! As we climbed the wide, shallow steps I noticed with delight more bits of marble, alabaster, part of a Corinthian pedestal and Grecian pots of all sizes stood at corners and curves of the steep path, placed with obvious loving care by an artist. Archways covered with flowering creepers shaded the paved path, translucent pale green grapes hung down, orange and lemon trees bending and heavy with dark green fruit, glowing pomegranates, sun-warmed peaches, apricots and yellow and red plums. The villas sat in an orchard rich with produce. It was an inviting place. Halfway up the slope we came across the makings of a swimming pool, a great rectangular gash in the ground on the only level piece of ground on the hillside. It would be magnificent when completed but was now an eyesore and a potential danger on a dark night.

After a more cautioned look we became aware of the debris everywhere; bits of corrugated iron sheeting, old bedsteads, chairs, drums, rusty buckets, broken bricks and piles of dirt and rags emitting a strong and nauseating stench of rotting fish. Villa Olga was badly neglected but it did not seem to matter for in the battle between neglect and the aesthetics of the garden — aesthetics had won. It just needed some loving care.

Then we saw the kittens. Four scraggy grey and white kittens with bat ears and spindly tails came yawning and stretching out of the shadows, wound themselves around our legs and talked with thin voices. Begging for attention. That did it! On discovering there was no one in any of the six villas we wrote down the phone number, extracted ourselves with great difficulty from the kittens — and left. It took us only a day to contact Mikalis the owner, who spoke no English and his urbane son Yiannis who did, and to move our belongings into one of the two-bedroomed villas near the top of the hill.

As we unpacked on that first day we kept looking at each other and grinning at our good fortune, for where else in the world can four people afford to live in such comfort; the rent was very reasonable, in such glorious surroundings where the sea breezes mingle with the scent of jasmine, roses and gardenias where apricots and plums fell to the ground as one brushed past; where the clarity of the sea was legendary and one could see thirty feet down, swim with turtles, chase octopus and dive down amongst shoals of sleeping fish suspended in the sunlit sea; where the mountains across the bay disappeared and reappeared several days later. Was it a trick of the light or the sipping of too much Cretan *raki* — that fire-water to which we had all taken? I hasten to add one small glass was sufficient to send my senses reeling and I seldom if ever, indulged in the second miniature glass.

To continue; where else can one live with unlocked doors and windows, safe in the knowledge that Cretans have respect for another's belongings and honesty prevails. And the family is all-important. Ours had expanded to include Mikalis who invited himself most evenings and arrived with arms laden with vegetables, fish for the cats and us, fresh bread, wine, litres of olive oil from his trees, and entertained us with a wonderful mix of Greek and very little English, his handsome face breaking into a broad smile, dark eyebrows lifting with amusement as we struggled to make ourselves understood, and his son Yiannis — our humorous and philosophical friend with his Byronic looks teaching us about Crete and Cretans.

CHAPTER FOUR

AN APPROACH IS MADE
I love this island

I awake at dawn and wander out across the tiled floor to the terrace at Villa Olga. The Thripte Mountains etched by an oriental brush seem to float on grey mist above the waters of Mirabello Bay. Calm. Tranquil. Softened and rested by the night, undisturbed by the bright stars and planets whose juxtaposition in the northern night sky is so strange to me since my night skies for fifty-five years have been many thousands of miles south in East Africa and Australia. The Southern Cross no longer features in the evening sky where it should be and this great arc above me seems to have more points of light. Or is it my imagination? I am transfixed by the sheer beauty of my surroundings. In the bay far below, scurries of wind pattern the dark surface of the sea where a boat lies at anchor. Sleeping still. To the southeast, the early sun catches the white buildings of Agios Nikolaos jutting out into the bay and outlines the elegant shape of one of the inter-island ferries. These ships arrive at dawn and disgorge their passengers — back-packers mostly — then take on a similar number and move silently out again to the next port of call. A canary in a cage in the Cretan household next door greets the awakening day as if undisturbed by the bars that enclose it; an answer floats back from the olive grove behind the villas — some other bird delighting in the dawn — and cockerels crow lustily, echoed by half a dozen from the little hamlet of Ellinika that lies just behind this property. Goats bleat. Someone drops a metal pot. Morning sounds.

The front door opens onto a flowering gardenia in a hundred-year-old pot according to Mikalis, its perfume mingles with that of the starry jasmine outside the original villa further down the terrace. The apricot has its branches propped up for it is so heavy with fruit that the soft plop as they fall is a familiar sound. Bowls of apricots lie untouched; the family will tire of this delectable fruit, though for breakfast a bowl of stewed apricots, Cretan yoghurt and honey flavoured with wildflowers was a favourite while we were living in the Green House, unsurpassed only by chunks of pale green cantaloupe, also called musk melon, and a dollop of sheep's yoghurt. Looking down the terraced gardens over the unfinished pool, the hibiscus shrubs that hang over the garden walls are opening their burgundy blooms towards the sun, and the deep purple bougainvillaea outside the villa on the same level as ours pulsates with radiant colour. The pomegranates glow. The day awakes in eastern Crete.

*

On my first morning at Villa Olga as my family lay sleeping I was moved to tears of gratitude and incredulity at the good fortune that had presented itself. I felt the strength of this great island — its age its tranquillity as it lay beneath me — and I knew that indeed I was meant to live here. As I surveyed the bay and its surrounding mountains it seemed to me that I had been waiting all my life for this moment and that this would be the end of my restlessness; that innate and ever-present knowledge that I was happy everywhere I went, yet something deep down, was not quite right. I have lived in many different places, raised four children, coped with fire and flood; the Mau Mau uprising in Kenya; left Africa and migrated to Australia, created gardens and homes in that order and certainly been supremely contented most of the time, yet something was missing. And now — leaning over the balcony confronted by water and mountains, barren hills and olive trees, hearing Greek voices, low in tone from the neighbour, I was filled with what the Greeks call κέφι, kefi, well-being, happiness. The word means so much it is considered to be 'beyond translation'. Everything seemed right. Nothing was missing. I had come home.

The next thing was how to approach Mikalis and persuade him that we wanted to remain here and take over the entire complex and run it ourselves. Following many family conferences, Julian finally came up with a sum that was viable and might be attractive to Mikalis if he would agree to the concept in the first place. I was not going to work *for* a Greek. I had been warned too often about the disasters that befell foreigners going into partnership with Greeks, but perhaps I could work *with* a Greek. We knew we could not buy property in Crete since it was classified as a 'border zone' due to its proximity to

Turkey; foreigners were forbidden to purchase land in border zones for fear of the Turks owning land on this island. The fear still looms large in the Cretan breast. Leasing seemed to be the obvious answer. Would he agree? We would have to draw up contracts but were there any English-speaking lawyers in Agios Nikolaos? It seemed unlikely, and my knowledge of Greek most certainly did not include the intricacies and nuances of legal terminology. We could but try. I was thrilled at the thought.

We approached Yiannis one evening and he seemed a bit suspicious. He asked us what our motives were and how was it that four of us could leave our lives and jobs in Australia and just move to another country? Were we fugitives from the law? We fell about laughing but he was serious, so we described our disenchantment with what had become 'our world' — city life, the stress factor, the cost of living, the pollution not only of the air but of the beaches, the increasing violence; we had no sense of belonging and for me perhaps more than the other factors, the loss of proximity to nature. A city balcony does not replace a garden. I have had a garden all my life until I moved to a flat in Sydney and I mourned its loss. These reasons and many more, Yiannis listened to with understanding and empathy. He would speak to his father and *θα δούμε,* tha thoume, we see, that had become his favourite expression when he was uncertain of the outcome. It transpired after many late evening talks on our terrace that Mikalis was over-committed and tired. He was not a well man. He and his father owned a bus which they both drove, a supermarket, and Mikalis was embarking on the construction of eight apartments in Agios Nikolaos. He welcomed the idea of us taking over Villa Olga provided he could keep his room, retain his interest in the garden and continue building the unfinished villa at the top of the property. What were our terms? We were bowled over! Never in our wildest dreams did we imagine that things would fall into our laps with such ease.

Over the ensuing weeks we negotiated a price and a three-year contract with the assistance of Sophia, a delightful lawyer who spoke excellent English. Mikalis agreed to complete the swimming pool though he argued good-naturedly about this until we made a stand and said, "No swimming pool — no deal," to which he finally agreed. Things took time but they eventually happened, *sigá-sigá,* slowly-slowly, was one of Mikalis' stock phrases when we showed our impatience at the delays, thinking with Sydney-based efficiency and urgency instead of the slower and eventually effective Cretan pace. It was after all this unhurried, unstressed philosophy and way of life we were seeking and it would take a while to accept and enjoy the Greek way — though I believe it was easier for me to adjust to this laid-back way of life having come from an East African background where absolutely nothing was done in a hurry.

*

"Καλημέρα, Michali" Kalimera Michali, Good morning — I hailed our landlord and friend one morning as he arrived in his little blue van, brandishing the daily plastic bag full of raw food for the family of cats and kittens that on hearing his van, would rush helter-skelter down the terraces to greet him frantically at the front gate. And what a feast he invariably brought for them; entire fish heads, chicken, noodles, vegetables, all of which they ate as if it were their last meal, even though we would surely feed them should he fail to appear; he called them with a curious swishing sound through pursed lips as he strode up the path like the Pied Piper followed by his eager coterie of cats.

"Οι γάτες έχουν ψίλου." I announced, which I thought translated to, "These cats have fleas!"

I hoped as I spoke, that he would not take this badly for this man loved his cats and fondled and stroked them with rough affection at every opportunity. He frowned, drew his heavy brows into a thick line across his forehead and picked up one of the kittens which, no longer half-starved and worm-ridden following several weeks of our treatment, had become nicely rounded and sleek with our care. The care included a bath in a warm tub after which we were surprised to find the coat *beneath* the red earth-tinged fur was white between the grey patches!

"Ναι ξέρω." Nai xero, Yes I know, he agreed, nodding his handsome head as he strode into his room to return with a tin of insect

spray which he sprayed onto each of the kittens, holding them by the scruff of the neck, laughing as they sneezed and protested, cuffing them affectionately as they struggled and spat at him, clawing at his hands. It was certainly a unique and effective way of de-fleeing cats; no expensive flea collars, no pills and no baths in toxic substances — just insect spray — probably more toxic than anything else. However, the fleas disappeared as fast as the kittens and they refused to approach him for days following the incident.

*

One of the first things we did was to decide on some method of identifying the six individual villas and studios; the concept of anglicising them with flower names repelled me though we could have had 'Hibiscus Villa' or 'Jasmine Villa' and even 'Smelly studio' since Mikalis opted to vacate his current noxious-smelling quarters and move his belongings to a storeroom, thus freeing up more space for rental accommodation. He announced this decision with aplomb and led us into his vacated rooms with pride saying they would be *polý kalá,* very good, for tourists when they were cleaned and painted. Reeling from the stench of unwashed clothing, dirty dishes and dried-up food covered with flies in the grimy sink and the stench of sewers and general decay, we surveyed the possibilities as we held our noses. This hitherto unseen space could make a pleasant studio with its upper-level double bed with a bathroom off to one side; the ground floor was long and narrow with a door at each end with just enough room for a small table and four chairs, a half-sized fridge and the usual two-burner stove standing on makeshift cupboards. One of the doors led into a tiny high-walled, paved courtyard with an outside brick oven where Mikalis and his family used to make bread when they lived in the original villa.

Shading the courtyard was a spreading apricot growing in red dirt littered with rubbish; this space was shared with the next villa down the hill whose back wall served as the dividing wall between the two. The only window was beside the bed and there was no view at all so the ambience was dark and somewhat claustrophobic, but we realised this would also mean the studio would remain cool as it got no direct summer sun — a big plus — and we would invite guests to take their meals out on the terrace around the swimming pool when it was completed. We decided to number — rather than name — the six villas and studios, starting at the bottom of the hill with the tiny villa on the right-hand side whose flat roof was the terrace of the largest villa immediately above it, and so on up the slope. Above the future pool to the left of the property was the spacious two-bedroom villa that we shared, its terrace being the roof of a narrow studio beneath, facing the bay and overlooking what would one day be the pool — lovely if Mikalis intended to keep his word.

*

Once we had taken over Villa Olga and had begun to advertise its charms in the UK and Australia I started to have qualms. Qualms about attracting more people to this lovely island that I wanted to remain exactly as it was and not over-crowded with foreigners. The little town of Agios Nikolaos still had its old-fashioned grocery shops, dusty and dirty with poor lighting and shelves crammed with all manner of things; sacks of flour full of weevils, paraffin lamps, packets of dried-up dates, old bottles of wine whose labels were so dust-covered they were illegible. These establishments were run by elderly Cretans, mainly sharp-eyed women always dressed in black — who until they got to know us — were somewhat aloof; not exactly unfriendly but cautious — but once they realised that we were here to stay, their demeanour changed almost overnight and we were always greeted with open and friendly interest. I liked the Cretans. They smiled a lot, were content with their lives. A happy people. They never hurried. They had time for each other, time to chat or just sit reflectively fingering their worry beads. Old men wrangled endlessly on their favourite subject — politics — and drank a lot of thick sweet coffee in the *kafenia,* cafés, while in summer the black-clad *yia-yias,* grandmothers, looked after the grandchildren while their daughters worked in tourism. The elderly, and I refer to women in particular, had a place in the whole scheme of things and were respected, not discarded. Crete was a place where one could age with dignity. They were never alone but kept active and involved in village life until they were too weak to get onto a donkey or harvest olives; then they peeled vegetables; worked with crochet and lace with their swollen arthritic fingers; or simply sat outside on rickety chairs against a sun-warmed wall, gossiping.

There were many pregnant women and numerous babies and children with gleaming black curls often seen on the front of their proud father's scooters, for Cretan men adored their children, especially the boys. I hoped these loveable characteristics would never change but I feared they might, and did I want to bring foreign visitors to this island to make a bit of money? No I did not. But we had to eat!

*

There is something special about swimming and snorkelling in these Mediterranean waters. I had read about the crystal-clear seas and thought, 'Oh yes, but I've swum off the East African and Queensland coasts and nothing can beat them' — yet strangely, those coral seas can offer almost too much colour and variety; the eye can become jaded, for a surfeit of anything eventually detracts from the individual. It is a bit like visiting large art galleries and museums that I enjoy, but there is just so much one can take in before the artworks and paintings merge into a blur and the need to sit down and have restorative caffeine becomes stronger than the desire to explore further treasures. The seas around Crete, whether they be the Libyan Sea in the south, the Cretan Sea to the north or the waters of Mirabello Bay where we swim most of the time, have no gleaming white and pink coral reefs and colourful fish are not plentiful, but the underwater world is magnificent — the essential difference being the distance you can see due to the extreme clarity of the water. As you dive down it is like opening a door onto a brilliant sunlit field stretching for miles with rocky shelves and outcrops, seaweed of varying colours and shapes waving in the breeze and the occasional human figure, one of us diving into view attached to a stream of bubbles. Turning upside-down you have a fish's impression of the surface of the water which resembles thick glass. Solid, except when breaking into a thousand bubbles on the rocks as the waves surge to and fro. The beauty of the undersea world cannot be satisfactorily described — it must be experienced. Using masks and simple breathing tubes we spent hours every afternoon drifting on the current to and from The Rock and discovering new creatures each time we swam. We become part of another world where time meant nothing — a weightless, floating dreaming world, silent and lit with shafts of sunlight and shadows that played on seaweed of saffron, mauve and greens of multiple shades and hues. An enchanted world.

Fish feed, some quite fastidiously others greedily, opening their mouths and pulling strongly on different types of seaweeds. One afternoon we watched a shoal of over a hundred sleek grey fish with yellow stripes and luminous eyes perform a kind of dance — touching the sandy bottom with their heads, then as they turned sideways they gleamed like silver. They appeared to be unaware of us humans floating above them and when we dived down they scattered briefly only to converge again and carry on as if nothing had interrupted their graceful game. We watched a small turtle, head high swimming towards us looking like a woman with a new perm trying not to get her head wet and we dived in from the rock in sheer delight and swam beneath watching the tiny flippers thrashing to and fro as it tried to combat the heavy swell. The turtle was in danger of being swept onto the jagged rocks so we picked it up gently and swam out to a deeper part of the bay and released it, but once more it headed deliberately shoreward and a wave washed it onto some rocks further along. It seemed pointless to interfere again. Mikalis told us that large turtles were often found in these waters. I would love to meet one.

One afternoon Mikalis expressed an interest in coming with us to The Rock. He had previously said he liked to swim "with his feet on the ground!" as he had a breathing problem and did not go out of his depth. We were delighted to have his company and he drove behind our scooters in his van, wearing a pair of shorts, a cloth cap and carrying a three-pronged spear; Poseidon personified. He also had a pair of goggles. Mikalis' concept of swimming was to poke around in the shallows while we dived and snorkelled, finding shards of what we believed to be exciting and ancient *amphora,* clay pots that he always dismissed with a hoot of derision and pretended to throw away. He then horrified us by spearing three sea urchins that abound in these waters which he proceeded to eat, first offering us some. Julian valiantly tried a piece which he said tasted like seaweed while we three girls swam in the opposite direction at great speed as Mikalis roared with laughter. I know they are considered to be a delicacy — but not for me! Cretans appear to eat most things, even the brightly coloured sea snake which we did not dive down to investigate, was pronounced by Mikalis to be *polý kalá,* very good to eat. The bay is a home for octopuses, some as large as dinner plates and others, tiny. And so vulnerable. These enchanting and highly intelligent ocean creatures cover the ocean floor at great speed, changing colour as their background alters, then hide beneath rocks and gather bits of rock and weed around them as camouflage for they are the target of all the spear fishermen who swim in these waters in the summer. When caught they are thrashed on the rocks — a hundred times Mikalis says — to tenderise them before being taken home for the evening meal. He cannot understand why we are appalled by this cruelty and only wish to observe and do not wish to kill; therein lies the essential difference between us — in many other ways we think and react in the same way.

I did some research on octopuses — or octopi — and learned that they are *cephalopods*, invertebrates which also includes squid and cuttlefish. *Cephalopod* is Greek for 'head-foot', which is appropriate since their limbs are attached directly to their head. They have eight arms and bulbous heads with huge eyes and they move with flowing grace and acuteness I had never seen before, and I have been swimming in oceans, both tropical and sub-tropical since I was three years old when my mother taught me to swim in the tepid waters of the Indian Ocean that embraces the East African coast and Dar es Salaam, my home. I was intrigued and overjoyed to be meeting these gentle and enchanting creatures for the first time as was the family as we glided along with the occasional need for a gulp of air, then down again; bubbles drifted up as we followed with flippers on our feet, along the sandy ocean floor with jagged coastal rocks and small caves that occasionally afford cover for the octopuses. We were all thrilled and intrigued after our first encounter.

*

CHAPTER FIVE

FLIGHT INTO EGYPT
Beware of pale Persians!

Francesca and I flew to Cairo from Crete via Athens, just a short trip, part of a 'freebie' offered by the airline from Australia, and although we knew July was the worst month to visit Egypt — no one, but *no one* goes to Egypt in high summer —but it was the only opportunity we had as Francesca was then flying to London and New York for a month before returning to her job in Australia in November. It was now or never. We agonised for days whether or not we should ignore the cost and go on a Nile cruise to those ancient places with their atmospheric names —Karnak, Abu Simbel, Luxor — or just get a taste and save *The Grand Tour* for another time when we saw how our business in Crete was faring. *Seize the day* has always been my philosophy and I was all for booking *The Grand Tour*, but for once prudence prevailed and we opted for the shorter, infinitely cheaper visit and needless to say, have regretted it since neither of us has enjoyed any tours at all much less *The Grand Tour* and I am re-writing this six years on!

Cairo – Rashid, our guide who has presumably been appointed by the travel agent to look after us for our three-day visit, meets us at the airport. Urbane, quick-moving he takes our passports asks for money and gives the lot to the man in uniform at passport control. We have no visas; fortunately no one asks to see them. I am surprised. We tried in Athens to get visas for our visit but the Egyptian Embassy was always closed and when we eventually got a tired voice at the end of the phone it said irritably, "You can get them in Cairo," and the phone was slammed down. The man at the passport control desk looks at the passports, takes the money and stamps something important on the pages and off we go at great speed following Rashid with obedience that doesn't go down well with me or my daughter.

First impressions — decidedly not at all good. For one thing we can barely see the city. It is smothered by a yellow pall of pollution worse than Athens which I thought was impossible, and desert sand, so a suggestion that we might like to go up the tower to "see Cairo" was vetoed. Ludicrous indeed as visibility is down to zero and remains so the entire duration of our stay. We become engulfed in traffic and pedestrians; camels with carts; camels without carts; donkeys; defunct traffic lights; soldiers; small boys pester pedestrians crying, *baksheesh, baksheesh* in their high-pitched, child voices; women in purdah; chaos; confusion; congestion; cacophony; and no discernible traffic rules. Our driver is negotiating at crazy speed along two-way lanes overtaking five vehicles whose drivers are all hooting and shouting at one another in guttural Arabic which is such a harsh language when shouted by an overheated, angry Arab. We have several very near misses and when I ask Rashid, who is not only a guide but also a driver, if there are many deaths on the road he waves his hand airily and replies, "Yes. Many. But too many people in Cairo anyway!" He grunts, or was it a laugh?

A sense of isolation and slight apprehension overwhelms me when for no given reason our hotel is swapped for a down-market version on the outskirts of Cairo; it is miles from anywhere and empty but for the staff who hover like vultures waiting to pounce. When we protest, Rashid dismisses our ifs and buts and says those were his instructions, so we give up.

Later, much later we are back in Crete and I am resuscitating the scribbled notes I wrote in Cairo.

On reflection, the reason for the hotel exchange became perfectly obvious; Rashid had put us in a cheap hotel and pocketed the difference! It *was* well appointed and clean but quite unnerving as good-looking young Egyptian males materialised at every turn and thrust their attention upon us; when we arrived at the lift three attendants offered their services, two of them assisted with our meagre luggage and then hung around for a tip. If we made a move, any move, someone was there to help us, open a door, move a plate, and enquire what we wanted. We were watched and waited on with an obsequiousness which made me shudder accompanied by the ubiquitous sentence; "You are welcome," as their almond eyes caressed my blonde daughter; she found it worrying, I just became irritated.

We made our way to the rooftop bar and discovered a swimming pool to our joy, but alas with the swimming pool and bar came half a dozen attentive men, mostly young and certainly good-looking. So attentive in fact we aborted the idea of a swim; hot and tired as we were we could not face that barrage of dark and invasive eyes that followed our every move. So we had a shower in our suite, raided the fridge and wonder why we have come at all!

"Tomorrow will be interesting," we agreed, there were places to go and things to see.

The three pyramids stand aloof and lofty above the chaos of Cairo as if they do not deign to recognise present-day Egypt but dream of the past in the stultifying heat of the sun. It is impossible to imagine the sheer size of the great stone blocks that look so insignificant in photographs. They are colossal. We went into Cheops, the largest of the three whose shadow is reputed to be three-quarters of a mile in length as the sun sets, but the claustrophobic narrow passages and an American female who slipped on a stair and started shouting hysterically put us off; a wave of fear overwhelmed me as I began to descend into the gloom and I turned hurriedly to find Francesca also turning round.

"Let's get out of here quickly!" We voiced in unison and hastened out into the blinding sun and vistas of bleached desert sands stretching away endlessly. Space and light. Light and space. These elements surround the pyramids and I was seized with a strong desire to find a camel and ride off into the distance to see what lies beyond the closest dune; to experience the desert. Not such a good idea as it turned out.

We chose the least pushy of the cameleers with his two gaudily decorated camels; mine was covered in heavy woven rugs, red, blue and gold with tassels, multi-coloured pom-poms around its head and had horrible huge green teeth and the most *dreadful* breath. Long streams of green slime hung from the corners of its mouth when it growled — and yes, they do growl. It swung its head around towards me and saliva flew into the air covering everything within yards. Now I really like animals but decided very quickly that I did not like this one and I could sense the antipathy was mutual. It did not like me either because it took one haughty look at me and let out a fearful bellow almost felling me with its halitosis. Then it farted.

I got on gingerly, thinking how much bigger a camel was than any horse I have ever ridden then I had a flash of Lawrence of Arabia

— actually Peter O'Toole as we all know — as he leapt onto his camel, white robes billowing and the jerky uneven way in which his camel got onto its four legs from a sitting position. I was puzzled as to which way I should lean to prevent myself from being hurled headlong into the arms of the greasy cameleer whose face now had the smarmy sneer that I read to mean, 'Now I've got them! I'll take these two stupid women into the desert and they will have to pay me to bring them back.'

All of this, including the vision of Lawrence ran through my mind when suddenly the camel heaved forward as he straightened his back legs and I was thrown forward with great force. A grunt, a release of stomach gasses and then I was tossed backwards as he adjusted his front legs. A stream of groans and snorts and more foul breath followed by an agonised bellow as he threw his head up into the air, green saliva flying everywhere and once again I was the recipient of his 'leavings' and felt seriously uncomfortable, filthy in fact.

He let out another snort and almost a groan and I wondered if he was in pain. Perhaps he had arthritis? What a lot of joints and what big ones in which to suffer pain.

Francesca was fine — a bit grubby of course, and we took photos of one another, much to the fury of the cameleer who cajoled and bullied us to allow him to take photographs of the two of us at a price; we had been forewarned. The more I refused the sulkier he became. We lumbered along behind him with a rather pleasant bouncing step and I thought I could get used to this and would love to go on and on.

The pyramids throw avenues of shade to the west and lower down the Sphinx which Rashid insisted on calling 'the Sphincter' looks on enigmatically. Palm leaves hang down limp with heat and Cairo is just visible through the haze. I figured if I chatted him up a bit then he might give us a longer ride so I said brightly,

"What do your camels eat?" He affected to not hear until I repeated the question.

"Alfalfa and papyrus," he spat through gritted teeth.

"And how long do they live?" I persisted encouragingly.

Again no reply. His step was becoming slower and slower and I suspected he was about to return to the base though we had only gone about twenty paces. He was not going to talk and he certainly wasn't going any farther so we followed him back furiously and he took our money without acknowledgement and turned away.

"What an unpleasant little sod!" We agreed and went to find a cool drink in a modern café with wide windows that overlooked the Sphinx which is enigmatic, secretive and not as large as I had expected. I was brought up with a sepia photograph of the Sphinx that hung on our sitting-room wall near the piano. Who took it, I wondered? I never asked my parents. And now here I was sitting within yards of it, so much smaller than I remembered but it is age, not size that matters and I was thrilled to be so close. So wise and so old. Proud too, looking out into the desert. We agreed the camel ride had not been the best of experiences, and interestingly I have subsequently heard these cameleers have been known to take riders into the desert and refuse to return until they have been paid large sums of money. Perhaps he saw the whites of my eyes?

*

We visited — at the insistence of our guide who like all guides everywhere obviously received the commission from every establishment to which he introduced us — a perfume merchant, whose shop stood in a slum street not far from the pyramids. On opening the carved wooden door we found ourselves in an Aladdin's Cave of riches; our senses besieged by wafts of heady perfume, plaintive eastern music played on unfamiliar instruments, carpeted floors, crystal chandeliers tinkling gently as cool air from ceiling fans disturbed them. Upstairs, behind delicately carved pale wooden screens inlaid with ivory and mother-of-pearl, velvet couches and armchairs with silk and satin cushions invited us to relax and forget the outside world. On the walls hung appliquéd reproductions of the friezes around Tutankhamun's' tomb; brightly tinted photographs and rows and rows of coloured perfume bottles of all shapes and sizes against walls of mirrors. Several colourful Egyptian women smiled encouragingly at us from behind their heavy make-up while carefully dusting these objects; kohl-lined eyes summing us up secretly and as they moved, anklets and bracelets jingled.

We had just come from the camels and I for one felt revolting. Sweaty, dirty, smelly, covered in green spit and wearing old clothes for the ride and pyramid climbing. I recall wondering if there was a scented bath of asses' milk behind the screen and wishing I could slide into it and get clean. Bath I did not have but the attentions of an utterly irresistible, pale Persian called Fouad, I did have. He established his bona fide very early on. He was Persian not Egyptian — as if that made any difference, after all he was 'still only a merchant' he said deprecatingly. He appeared as if conjured up by a genie, dressed in flowing robes of palest ivory, gossamer-fine yet opaque; pure silk socks and superb Italian leather pumps on his slender feet. His hands and fingers were long and graceful with beautifully manicured nails, slightly tinted. He was a gorgeous man. We sat in our camel odour and filthy clothes as he wooed us both with silken vowels and of course, in perfect English. Naturally, he was only interested in Francesca whom he called his 'queen' which we thought highly amusing. We found it difficult not to giggle however he was wise enough to know that to win the daughter he had also to win the mother. He poured compliments over us like warm velvet, gazing into our faces with his caressing tawny eyes as he proceeded to dab perfumes onto various parts of Francesca's anatomy with suggestive comments, though voiced in the most gentlemanly manner to which one could not possibly take offence.

"Thees one will make your lover *mad!*" he whispered dabbing 'Gardenia' on her upper arm, near the sensitive erotic zone I noticed. She squirmed, green eyes showing some amusement and not a little surprise. We knew what was coming next.

"And thees one will make sure he is more mad. With *love* and *passion* you know," he crooned, dabbing it on her brown knee. Francesca's eyes grew larger and slightly apprehensive.

"Eet is called L'amour."

Oh yes, I thought. Bet I can guess what the next line will be. Leaning over my daughter he put his smooth, cologned face next to hers and half-whispered, "Do you have a lover and where ees he?"

Before she could answer, "and thees" as she crossed her legs hurriedly avoiding his probing fingers as he headed for her inner thigh but had to make do with the outer one.

"Thees perfume is called Mid-night. Are you busy tonight at midnight?"

She giggled and moved closer to me, reeking of perfume. I detected a slight hesitation in his manner; he was wasting his time and he knew it.

"Yes lovely, I like that one," murmured Francesca and she stood up rapidly and crossed the vast room to inspect one of the ornate rugs hanging on the wall. Things were getting a little out of hand; she looked at me with wide imploring eyes.

"I'll have a small bottle of the Gardenia and L'amour, please," she said.

He turned and looked closely at me, his perfume overwhelming as he stroked his narrow moustache with a long elegant, finger. He wore many rings.

"And you, madam?"

"Unfortunately I'm allergic to perfume," I said, "otherwise I'd have bought up the whole shop."

I laughed. Actually, I'd have bought him had I been able to but I knew I was facing fierce competition from my daughter. He was happy to be photographed with Francesca and urged me not to hurry as I struggled with her camera. I've never been good with cameras.

"I will talk to my queen," he murmured as he hugged her. She appeared to enjoy the intimacy as he suggested I take several more, but a small shriek and a quick move away from his wandering hands indicated the photographic call was over.

We had tea in porcelain cups and admired the photographs of him with Dior, Coco Chanel and other big names from the international world of perfume; he had his gardens by the Nile he said and exported the concentrate all over the world. He was, he told us, "Very famous all over the world," and as we left, he smiled or was it a grimace? His pale eyes remained lifeless — we had wasted his time!

*

We packed a lot into our three days; visited the magnificent mosque of Sultan Hassan with its marble quadrangle and fountain housed in a delicate tracery of marble, and inside listened to the chanting of the worshippers beneath the enormous chandelier. One evening we boarded the gold and ornately decorated steamer *The Nile Pharaoh* and cruised silently up the great river while we wined and dined and watched a bored and bad belly dancer gyrate to an out-of-tune three-piece band. It was third-rate entertainment but as we slid past the darkening banks with their villages framed by date palms, unchanged by time, we felt elated and it made up for the twentieth-century tourist rubbish that was being inflicted upon us. The waiters were attractive and not obsequious and not over-attentive towards my daughter which was a relief. The excellent and tasty fare was presented on a grand scale and served on a central table that ran the entire length of the dining salon that held at least a hundred-and-fifty tables, though only about twenty were occupied. The wide variety of delectable dishes was kept hot on burners and beautifully arranged between bowls of fragrant frangipani, orchids and other exotic flowers.

We sat opposite a stilted Egyptian family with an incredibly well-behaved child. They ate a different meal to ours and hardly breathed a word to one another, and made no effort to communicate with us though we tried initially. We would have liked to have been at a table where there was lively conversation, even if we couldn't understand it for we heard no English, only Italian, French and Arabic. On our return to our hotel that night, we noticed several armoured vehicles touring the streets filled with very young men in uniform all sporting sub-machine guns. How young do they recruit men in Egypt, I wondered. They were all rather excited and in my opinion were too immature to be handling lethal weapons. I felt distinctly uneasy in the presence of so many armed personnel; during the day all the major government buildings and the embassies — these I could accept — bristled with uniformed men, guns and dogs. I was glad I lived in peaceful, non-violent Crete.

I was dying to see the new Opera House — sadly the old one had burnt down a few years earlier — and we managed to get tickets. The building was plain and rather stark and not my idea of an opera house at all but then I am not really of the twentieth century in my tastes. There we were subjected to scrutiny and our bags were checked by more men with guns, and mixed with the elite of Cairo's embassy crowd; the Brits with their clipped voices and laid-back manners accompanied by understated wives with straight fair hair; gorgeously dressed Italians; Orientals in heavy brocade outfits; but the Egyptian women occupied all our interest. Like over-stuffed birds of paradise, they moved among the crowd wearing the most colourful if outlandish clothes in the latest fashions; suits with huge padded shoulders and appliquéd lapels; blouses and dresses covered with embroidery, glitz, glitter and sequins; and the most amazing multi-coloured shoes and hair decoration; make-up so thick you could have scraped it off with a knife.

Spain's top flamenco dancer, a tiny ageing man whose name I forget, with his troupe of dancers, the women with their strong gypsy features, brilliant eyes and supple bodies and the tightly-trousered men — invariably better looking than the women — danced and twirled to the fantastic guitars and raw voices as they thumped the floor with their shiny boots. Exciting stuff. I needed to visit the bathroom but was not permitted to leave the auditorium until the interval. Pity the pregnant women I thought. At the interval, we were astounded to find ourselves pushed and shoved and almost trodden on by the members of the audience who so monopolised the bar we were unable to get a drink and they devoured all the nuts and tit-bits and generally behaved like hoodlums. I was astonished and assured my daughter that we had never behaved like that in similar circumstances in the early days in Dar es Salaam!

And of course — the museum. Mere words fail if one attempts to describe the sumptuousness of the Egyptian dynasties; Tutankhamun's' treasures glittering with gold and precious stones, lapis-lazuli, ivory; the colossal gold sarcophagus and tombs within;

the delicacy of his favourite chair superbly carved; riches beyond description and beauty in such abundance I wondered, as I often do, what has happened to the world since those days. Those skilled and ancient civilisations such as the Pharaohs, Minoans, Aztecs and the Chinese left such exquisite works of art depicting their way of life and beautifying themselves and their surroundings, whereas we appear to be hell-bent on total destruction and I suspect that all that will be left of our 'civilisation' is a damned great hole in the ground.

*

Finally, out of the yellow cloud of Cairo and into the blue skies of Crete which already felt like home, though we had only been there a few months. The visit to Cairo had been interesting, but too short by far and the upper reaches of the Nile unvisited — perhaps next time?

CHAPTER SIX

CRETAN LIFESTYLE
Settling in

We wanted a different way of life and we have certainly achieved our aims! Where we once all had cars we now have two scooters and 'dink' one another — the word is an Australian term meaning to carry a second person on a bike or scooter. This gives us the freedom to follow intriguing goat tracks to high places inaccessible to a car; to explore crumbling and deserted villages; investigate white churches and chapels that are always on mountain tops; to find new rocks from which to dive; hidden bays with pale sand so fine it squeaks between the toes. Secret places. There is nothing as exhilarating as being on a scooter with your hair blowing about with the sound of the wind in your ears, hurtling over the saddle of a hillside to spy a tiny bay and little fishing villages white in the sun, spread out before you. Even the hottest day does not seem unbearable when you are flying along with the world at your feet and the time to explore.

Things really are very different. Where in Sydney we lived in flats or houses with balconies and led separate lives we now temporarily share one spacious villa. Francesca and I share one bedroom; we keep our clothes in one small cupboard, a hat rack and use three waste-paper baskets for our undies. It doesn't worry us one bit. For one thing our wardrobe is reduced to shorts, t-shirts and swimming costumes though when winter comes we will need more clothes and certainly more space. When we venture into Agios Nikolaos or Elounda, our nearest coastal town in the opposite direction for an evening meal, or try out one of the many lively discos, the trend is casual. No serious dressing up.

At the moment we are living in Villa Five, the second largest, newest villa with two bedrooms, a lavatory and shower; a combined and spacious living-dining room leads onto a vast terrace with what must be one of the most spectacular views on the planet. Furnishings in all the villas and studios are simple — basic really and not entirely comfortable — but perfectly adequate when the guests spend practically no time at all indoors. In between guests we 'sleep around' and try out each of the villas to see what is needed, how comfortable they are and I have moved into Villa Four, which is my favourite so far. It is one of the oldest villas and has a rustic Cretan charm which the more recent additions lack. Brilliant hibiscus and bougainvillaea and ubiquitous citrus trees along a short path shade its approach and inside, a dark wooden lintel supports the doorway into the small living/dining-room where all the walls are white. With its simple Cretan furnishing, wooden beams and decorative door it has an attractive fireplace of carved stones inlaid with interesting bits of old pottery, the terrace is huge and looks out over the blue expanse of the bay where as I write I can see a yacht with white sails drifting very slowly, for the wind has dropped.

Julian and Nathalie also 'sleep around'. Currently they are trying out the luxurious Villa Two which is twice the size of the others and the original villa on the property. There are three bedrooms, a vast living room with fireplace, decent full-sized armchairs and a couch, dining area at the far end and it actually has a small bath consisting of two levels so one has to sit with one's legs down — but it's a bath nonetheless and the only one in the complex. The kitchen is large and separate with a full-sized fridge and a very ancient stove whereas all the other villas and studios have two-ring gas burners. The back door of the kitchen leads onto the small courtyard, which is shared with what we call Studio Three, that used to be Mikalis' pad. I've slept the occasional night in tiny Villa One which nestles against the hillside immediately below the terrace of Villa Two. It faces an enchanting paved courtyard surrounded by roses, bougainvillaea, pristine perfumed gardenias shaded by a lustrous pomegranate with glowing fruit that hangs down like lanterns, a fig tree, a mature and fruit-heavy peach and citrus trees. Below the supporting stone wall I can see the tops of silver-grey olives and below that terrace, the coast road that was so noisy as summer progressed — but somehow it didn't seem to matter as everything around us was a-quiver with life and fun and activity. Besides, once my head hit the hard pillow I was always asleep within seconds — tired out and sublimely happy with each day's experiences. How lucky can one be?

There is a stone table in the courtyard where I sit with my typewriter with my brain almost dizzy with the perfumes and shades of Nature's bounty. What a heavenly place this is. All the villas were designed by Mikalis and vary slightly in style which makes them so interesting. At the top of the property up the hill is a hideous concrete shell that Mikalis has announced is to be his pride and joy; he envisages a larger and more modern interior with two spacious bedrooms, the usual living rooms plus a fireplace built by the finest stonemason in Crete. He rolls his brown eyes as he describes his dream villa, but I immediately wonder how long the finest stone mason will last! I ask him when he is planning to start building, rather than actually completing this structure and he says πολύ σύντομα, *polý sýntoma,* which I gather means 'very soon'. I can see drachmas spinning around in his scheming brain; this means we will have seven places to rent out and more villas to clean. Oh woe is me! I hope we can keep them all full but the cleaning will be a nightmare.

*

There is an unusual show of energy between the midnight departure of guests and the arrival of the next occupants an hour later by taxi from the airport; a thorough dusting is always needed, bed linen is whipped off the beds, ash-trays cleared, the loo bin emptied, shower recess scrubbed, the fridge and kitchen top scrubbed and a mop is run over the stone and marble floors at high speed. Within fifteen minutes or so there is no sign that anyone has occupied that villa at all. We are becoming adept at this and all contribute to the flurry before settling down to our normal, unhurried way of life. We have been fortunate that in the first six weeks of leasing Villa Olga, it has been filled with a succession of delightful French and Italian visitors. Six Irish back-packers arrived out of the blue; luckily we had accommodation for them. They were thrilled to discover this green oasis after a disappointing visit to Egypt and weeks of hard work on a kibbutz in Israel. They will be back they say, with their gentle, lilting accents. Friends from England and Australia seem to arrive each week and we have had some memorable parties already with the promise of more to come.

Julian is worried that I tend to forget that this is a business and not just an extension of our new and enjoyable regime; he tells me that I should *not* keep on inviting guests to coffee, drinks on the terrace at dusk and impromptu meals that are costing us money. But how does one separate business from pleasure when one has never been in business before? I hate the idea of relating life to income but I know he is right — still, I have no idea how to indicate to good friends that they are expected to contribute when my instinct is to share what we have. One of the problems is that we are seven kilometres away from the nearest shops — exactly halfway between Elounda and Agios Nikolaos — and most of our guests arrive by plane in the middle of the night. We provide a free welcome basket that consists of coffee, tea, sugar, milk, fruit, a bottle of wine, fresh bread or rolls with butter and jam — but this only keeps the wolf from the door until they have arranged their own transport or found their way to one of the two ports. There are no supplies to be had locally so we decide we will have to start a shop — but later on.

*

We have been here for about ten weeks and I notice the change in us all; not only the physical changes for we are all trimmer, browner and decidedly stronger — but changes more profound than the superficial. Francesca — the eldest of my three daughters — looks ten years younger than her thirty-four years, the signs of strain now replaced by a more relaxed and happier demeanour, though effervescent as of old. My son Julian is more outgoing — more volatile — his inner strength now visible from the exterior for Greece is undoubtedly a man's world and the man must be *seen* to be a man. My French daughter-in-law Nathalie says she feels totally at ease for the first time since leaving her childhood home in Morocco; her dimples show more often and her flawless, smooth skin glows a golden brown. She has an amazing supply of energy and has taken over the task of caring for the garden when Mikalis is not around; digging and weeding and sighing when it is hot but always with her enchanting smile as she unfolds her tired back. And as for me — I don't know what changes the family sees but I awake with the calm and contented knowledge that 'all's well with the world' and it is many, many years since I have experienced that inner peace. The most welcome change is being able to rest when I am tired instead of urging myself on and on beyond my physical capabilities; it is absurd to be so grateful for what surely should be my right. Nowadays we may feel tired, but it is from strenuous purely physical work like painting the villas, cleaning, clearing the garden or possibly even too much swimming and sun; it is healthy tiredness, the right kind from which one recovers after a good night's sleep. And it does not matter if we are not up at seven the next day; there is no Sydney Harbour Bridge to cross, no traffic to hold one up — just another bright and beautiful day in Crete. Mind you on occasions we suffer slightly from the aftermath of imbibing too much firewater from the night before with visiting friends, but there are no headaches the morning after, just a curious cotton-wool occupation of the brain cells which refuse to function effectively until we drink our first cup of good Greek coffee *ελληνικό καφέ, Elliniko kafé.* Thick as mud.

We have already made some good friends. The two women in the post office, initially somewhat cool and withdrawn, now light up when one of us goes in for the mail — if there are no letters in poste restante they look quite melancholy and say encouragingly, *Ισως αύριο,* Maybe tomorrow, or on handing us our precious letters, they smile and share our delight for there is empathy between us. Mail from the remaining family and friends in Australia and other parts of the world is important to us as we have no other means of communication. The baker's wife with tired eyes is a tiny woman who knows our preferences; she finds us a wholemeal loaf often straight from the heart of the oven; the price is ridiculously low, seventy drachmas for the largest size. She treats us like favoured customers. And the elderly couple in the photographic shop who insist on giving us cups of Greek coffee, the best in Agios Nikolaos they tell us, accompanied by glasses of ice-cold water — they are always so busy but never too busy to be hospitable.

In the tiny village of Ellinika which lies on the crest of the hill overlooking Villa Olga, groups of wizened *yia-yias,* with eyes full of the wisdom of their years, sit against the sun-hot walls of tiny stone cottages; their knotted hands are always busy, doing crochet, lacework, de-husking nuts and preparing vegetables. Village life continues blessedly untouched one minute away from our holiday villas; black-eyed children run, skip and play in the narrow street; cats sit hunched on rooftops catching the last rays of the dying sun; men drink ouzo at the *kafenion*, fidget with their worry beads and argue about politics or the recent scandal involving the latest prime minister and the price of grapes. It has always been thus. On occasions we take the road through the village instead of the main road, and the villagers wave and call out καλημέρα, kalimera, good-day, and the old woman who milks the goats and has a beard to match does not seem to mind our noisy scooters; the animals also find them intriguing and stop chewing momentarily as we pass by. We were initially sensitive about disturbing the tranquillity of the villages but far from disturbing the inhabitants, it is evident that we provide them with interest and stimulus. Word has got around that this mad family with no car who double-up on scooters is here to stay and we are always greeted with genuine warmth and friendliness. We have a sense of belonging, of being accepted.

One of the best things about Agios Nikolaos our main town is its modest size; with a population of less than nine thousand — sans tourists — it does not take long to get to know the locals. Our Wednesday visit to the weekly market that spreads itself over the car park and several streets below the hospital is an expedition we look forward to — albeit a hot one even though we leave the villas very early.

Before coming to Crete I was under the impression that Greek food was unpalatable. Not so! The markets are an eye-opener with stalls of magnificent vegetables and fruit extolled mostly by gipsies with their harsh voices, brown eyes flashing and bracelets jingling. Trucks come from western Crete piled high with citrus; from the south filled with cucumbers, sweet tomatoes of a flavour untasted previously, artichokes, avocados, gigantic white cauliflowers; masses of fruit, even guavas in summer; great vats full of snails that persist in climbing out much to the frustration of the stall-holder; the grey-eyed man who sells spicy village sausages and half a dozen varieties of village cheeses also has sheep's yoghurt in desirable terracotta bowls. Wonderful in this age of plastic. Not only food but piles of clothing, trays of shoes, bikinis, hats, linen and kitchen utensils have found their way into every one of our little kitchen nooks in the villas. We found white lacy curtaining which we have sewn by hand and put up at the small windows in the studios to help keep out the blazing sun — but not to hide the views of the bay.

After the market, the ride back up the winding hill on our scooters with our knapsacks laden to capacity, then breakfast on the terrace overlooking the glistening Bay of Mirabello with the serrated edges of the Thripte Mountain range mirrored in the morning calm. The need to sit and cogitate takes over and I find it hard to drag myself back from my reverie for this is a land where dreams come true. Our eating habits have changed though I have always eaten a lot of salads and vegetables; we are now almost vegetarian, a choice easy to make as the vegetables of Crete are renowned for their flavour and excellent quality and red meat loses its appeal in hot weather. Sadly, fish is expensive and has now become a luxury.

Mikalis has introduced us to παξιμάδια, *paximathia,* double-baked chunks of dark bread favoured by shepherds and villagers alike which resemble rusks. These traditional rock-hard rusks have been around since early Minoan and Egyptian times. The only way to make them edible is to dip them briefly under a running tap, douse liberally with olive oil, preferably from Mikalis' trees, salt and pepper, sprinkle with oregano and a squeeze of lemon juice from the trees at Villa Olga. Eaten alone, these rusks are interesting but we have devised a more rewarding and substantial *paximathia* salad by including finely chopped cabbage, feta cheese, olives, tomatoes in quarters, onion and capsicum rings, olives and cucumbers and not forgetting dried oregano. The mouth-watering bowl of colourful ingredients invites a final sprinkling of olive oil from Villa Olga's trees naturally and lemon juice. Tradition tells us that it is the man who is head of the table and he mixes the salad before passing it around to his hungry family and friends. Food for the gods and the goddesses!

I did some research as to how these rusks came about and one of the legends tells us that they were named after a Byzantine monk called *Paximus* who improved on an ancient recipe that today is a living tradition. *Paximathia,* Cretan rusks are double-baked and made with whole grain barley flour; the fibre allegedly makes them beneficial to one's health by reducing cholesterol levels. I discovered the dough can come from any number of other sources such as wheat, rye, corn, carob and chickpea flour, or from a combination thereof.

The Greek word μεζέδες, mezethes, appetisers or *hors d'oeuvres* the French term, is a selection of small dishes of almost every delectable morsel one can imagine. When having a meal in one of the tavernas we invariably order a selection of Cretan *mezethes,* with a glass of something and seldom order anything else since there is no room left! We have counted as many as ten different mouth-watering bowls of new and delicious offerings on our table yet there is not even a crumb left for the inquisitive ducks and geese that hover around when we are dining by the deep waters of the lake.

The Cretans have their traditional recipe of these rusks that they also call ντάκος, dakos, similar to our recipe but is a more filling dish; it consists of the round *paximathia* about five inches in diameter topped with grated ripe tomatoes, crumbled feta or *mizithra* cheese, black olives, salt and pepper and sprinkled with oregano and finally liberally dribbled with virgin olive oil and lemon juice.

Breakfast is a casual affair eaten at different times or not at all depending on the mood of the individual and the cleaning demands to be completed before afternoon and evening arrivals. What could be more delectable than a bowl of creamy sheep's yoghurt, thyme honey from the hillsides dribbled onto slices of sweet melon, or apricots, peaches or plums from our trees? Lunch, unless it is a picnic on our rock, consists of a salad of some sort — either *paximathia* or with tuna or sardines or one of the sharp village cheeses followed by whatever fruit we can find in the market, or from our trees. The evening meal somehow happens with little prior discussion among the four of us though Nathalie's expertise regarding flavours and ideas is unsurpassable. Mostly it is a vegetable dish occasionally livened up with local spicy sausages or salami, both very tasty.

Sometimes we have omelettes flavoured with shallots or tomatoes and as a treat, Cretan chips cooked in our own olive oil which is a darkish green in colour with a flavour hard to describe; somehow it is reminiscent of the earth and the trees from whence it springs. There is something very special about using oils pressed from olives grown on familiar trees; we also use it on our skin after a swim and on our hair as the best conditioner after too much salt and sun. Step aside Vidal Sassoon and others — pure olive oil reigns at Villa Olga!

One of our favourite meals when we feel the need to splash out is barbecued fish — a whole fish — cooked over the open coals in the Cretan way with Mikalis as master chef. The scales are left on to keep the flesh together and Mikalis sprinkles the fish with a mixture of olive oil, lemon juice and herbs while it is cooking, filling the night air with a mouth-watering aroma which almost drives the kittens mad. We prepare fresh salad and crusty bread and have difficulty waiting for the firm white fish to be brought to the table where it is washed down with good Cretan wine. Slices of pale green cantaloupe as sweet as sweet round off the meal before coffee, after which we sit silent and replete, satisfied with our world and once again acknowledging our good fortune. We are told that the waters around Crete are almost fished out hence the cost, so this treat is rare and undoubtedly more enjoyable because of it.

There is no set routine to our days. No one wears a watch because it doesn't matter what time it is unless we are expecting visitors, and this freedom after being pinned to time and deadlines for so many years is indeed a relief beyond description. We eat when we are hungry — usually between one and three — hurtle on our scooters down to The Rock for the afternoon and return about five for a short siesta, then work till dark which in high summer is well after nine o'clock. Then, when the evening has cooled and the cicadas have gone to sleep, we have our meal on the terrace under the great arc of the night sky with its configuration of stars still not familiar to me.

We read a great deal and brought a few good books with us and have been surprised to find an excellent bookshop owned by a quiet and charming woman called Anna Karteri in Agios Nikolaos, on the road down to the port; she has a good selection of books in English on Greece and Crete, which is what we are interested in. These will keep us going until our boxes arrive from Australia though where we shall put everything when they arrive I have no idea. We play chess, Scrabble, cards, listen to music and have time to dream. This rare commodity in our previously harried and hurried lives is something we relish for we were indeed world-weary human beings when we arrived. Now our minds are uncluttered by external trivia; we don't buy newspapers though there are English newspapers at some of the stands in town and we don't listen to the radio at all except in search of music, but the reception is bad. We have switched off totally and for the moment this is necessary; we may well crave these things later but for the present, we are discovering more about ourselves and each other and revelling in being close to nature and the people of Crete.

CHAPTER SEVEN

WE HAVE OUR MEDICALS
Magic in our lives

"You will be required to have extensive medicals," they all said and I can't remember who 'they' were now but several people warned us of this impending experience that we who would live in Greece, would have to undergo. How extensive were the tests we asked tremulously? Should we mention various complaints and problems from which we suffered and if we didn't — would they find out? I hasten to add that basically there was nothing wrong with any of us, but one is always apprehensive of the unknown.

So the day came. We would go to the Public Office in town to get our list of tests and do what had to be done. The first part was relatively easy except that no one in the Public Office least of all the bored receptionist, spoke English. My Greek yet again proved to be inadequate although I had practised a few suitable sentences before our visit. These came in handy when a severely crippled man up some stairs finally led us to a woman who *did* speak a little English. She gave us the authorisation papers that were all in Greek and directed us to the hospital up the hill. All this had taken so long that we were compelled to stop at the little coffee place halfway up the slope and reinforce our flagging spirits with ice-cold *café frappé* and oven-crisp *σπανακόπιτες*, spanakopitas, cheese and spinach pies. Thus fortified we climbed onto our scooters once more and zoomed up the hill to the hospital.

Once again the receptionist spoke no English which I found odd since so many English ex-patriots worked in Agios Nikolaos through the summer, and the thousands of tourists who descended on this part of eastern Crete were predominantly English and in the habit of falling off their hired scooters necessitating a visit to the hospital. *Surely* she spoke some English? But no — she lifted her eyes and chin to the ceiling in the now familiar Greek negative. She did, however, manage to take three thousand drachmas from each of us, gave us receipts and several pieces of paper and waved us vaguely in the direction of the crowded corridors farther along. We made our way to the far end where a man was shouting and waving his arms about in great agitation, watched in astonishment by both staff and out-patients. This live Greek drama went on for about five minutes until a white-coated man presumably a doctor appeared and led him away, an arm firmly placed over the man's shoulders. We wondered if he was an escapee from some mental institution or merely a frustrated Cretan making his presence felt. A woman who was also waiting, enlightened us and said the man had made an appointment to see the doctor and had been kept waiting two hours. "She is not happy," the woman remarked with a wry smile, making the habitual error of all Greeks with the pronoun. An understatement to be sure. She also told us that we were at the wrong end of the hospital so we fought our way back to our initial point of entry through crowds of noisy outpatients. It was unbearably hot and stuffy and there was nowhere to sit; even a hard bench would have been welcome. Eventually, after approaching half a dozen members of staff with my well-practised *"Μιλάτε αγγλικά?"* Milateh anglika? Do you speak English? we found a doctor who could answer our questions; he looked tired and a bit distraught and I wondered how many hundreds of people like us wasted his valuable time each day. He sighed as he looked at our papers and told us to return to the other end of the hospital once more.

"That's it!" We spoke with one voice and stomped out of the hospital, leapt onto our scooters and headed for the healing cooling ocean, having had the foresight to bring our costumes with us. What the hell — we would try again tomorrow. Maybe!

Next morning, fresh and enthusiastic we arrived early hoping to beat the rush. But no! We waited an hour to see the dermatologist whilst families pushed and shoved and leaned on his door trying to beat the queue; he had a list of names which he called out and each time he opened the door there was a surge of people that he politely but firmly requested to sit down and await their turn. The ensuing arguments with the specialist reached heated levels and the noise factor was astonishing, but we were in Greece. The dermatologist, when we were finally ushered in en masse, was an astonishingly handsome and charming doctor with whom we three girls fell instantly in love. *Now* I can understand the rapt following of the medical series on television having found that doctors can be delicious even in real life, it is just that I haven't come across them that often. My son also had his thrill as the assistant was a glamorous brunette with red nails, a short skirt and more length of leg than usual displayed as she sat on top of the desk, chewed gum, filed her nails and took a long telephone call while the dermatologist examined us.

Next — the blood and urine tests plus X-rays. We walked the full length of that now horribly familiar corridor several times before discovering where to go by which time it was too late. Both pathology and X-ray closed at eleven-thirty for some extraordinary reason. Come back tomorrow, we were advised. Early. Over another *café frappé* sitting on flimsy chairs we worked out that if one test took three hours then we probably had another twelve hours of waiting. We purchased our sample bottles from a chemist and headed home. Early next morning, before taking turns to sit on the loo to collect our samples we spent some time trying to work out which the 'third movement' was. The written instructions on the samples of body fluids and solids to be taken first thing in the morning read:

'Samples from the first, second and third movements to be taken etc'…which sounded more like a symphony than a pathology test.

It was later on that evening, as I sat chewing almonds from our laden trees on the terrace above the swimming pool that I had my first doubts about living in Crete. I had always known it would not be easy, but the language barrier the last two mornings had proved almost insurmountable — but not totally of course — my habit of arguing with myself coming to the rescue once again. But I felt so vulnerable, like seaweed in the tide being pulled this way and that from one end of the corridor to the other. I could read the signs but did not understand them. I felt I had failed miserably and went to bed silently and not as positive as usual. Had my dream been foolish?

A good night's sleep and the gentle glow of dawn over the bay dispelled my gloom and next morning we were at the hospital by eight o'clock with our samples, the procurement of which had caused some merriment earlier on. We had our blood taken, chest X-rays done and were out of the hospital in under two hours. Amazing.

All that remained was the awesome psychological tests that had to be done in Heraklion, an hour's drive to the west. It had crossed my mind that these tests might take a bit of time and that we should make appointments, but someone said we could just turn up — which we did — only to be told that we had to make appointments and come back next week! This, after hiring a car especially for the purpose. We sought the usual solace, Greek coffee and this time, our favourite *bougatsa,* a sweet and delectable pastry filled with soft cheese and sprinkled with cinnamon after which we wandered around the dusty, noisy streets, visited the market then returned home in a borrowed kind of jeep. I sat in the back with a scarf around my head feeling a bit like the queen at an equestrian event; Francesca was in New York by then while Julian and Nathalie bounced around in the front seats; my son was driving, holding on for dear life as there were no doors. We were blown to blazes but it was exhilarating.

Back to Heraklion the following week in the same borrowed car. Another hard bench in a hot corridor sitting too close to a woman in black who had not washed since she went into mourning twenty years earlier, or so she told me. Nathalie went to sleep. After an hour, a woman in a white starched uniform called us all in and we sat down in front of a tired and myopic young man who appeared to have neck problems. Tension, I thought.

'Physician, heal thyself.'

He asked for our passports while we sat on the edge of our hard seats and waited, the words of warning ringing in our ears.

"They are really extensive tests you know and you'll begin to wonder why you have to go through all of these. But don't worry, everyone has to."

The psychiatrist looked at my passport briefly then asked my name and age. Funny, I thought. He can speak English therefore he must be able to read English so he already knows my name and age. Is it a trick question? To me there was no reply other than the obvious one, which I gave him. Then he asked why I wanted to live in Crete. I don't recall what I said apart from the fact that I already loved the island and wanted to become part of it. Once again thinking that this must be a trick, a trap, and he would analyse my response, find hidden meanings and pronounce me unfit for permanent residency. My reply was therefore not my usual spontaneous one but something more guarded. His expression was impassive as he moved on to Nathalie and Julian and asked them the same questions. Sighing deeply he signed the papers on his desk, handed them to the woman in white who had begun to hover, returned our passports and shook hands as he dismissed us. His hand was limp and floppy. Was he *really* a psychiatrist or just someone posing as one I wondered.

We were sent upstairs with our signed papers to the secretary who spoke English and asked her what came next; she looked surprised, stamped our papers once more and replied,

"He says you are all very healthy," and that was that.

We celebrated that evening on our balcony with Mikalis. For us the first hurdle was over, there would undoubtedly be more but come hell or high water we would be staying at Villa Olga.

"*Stin yiamas,*" to our health we cheered and clinked glasses, eyes meeting in keeping with sound, one of the five required senses when having a drink as the evening light turned the mountains across the bay to deep plum. More magic in our lives.

*

Speaking of magic — I have been reminiscing on the similarity between the relaxed Cretan way of life and my many years in East Africa where the overwhelming atmosphere was one of a gentle pace with gentle people, that is until politics and confusion altered the scene and it became obvious we should leave, however painful it would be. We packed up, caught a flight to Aden then boarded a liner to Australia and now — on this still night everyone has gone to bed and my middle-aged brain has flashed back to a magical episode with the same two children who are now spending their days working like Trojans, in our new venture at Villa Olga. How time flies. Francesca vividly remembers our meeting a herd of giraffes along the old slave trail, but two-year-old Julian was more interested in his thumb. The year was 1958.

We were driving from the coast to the hinterland through a vast region known as the Itigi Thicket, a huge expanse of *miombo*, dry forest, consisting of dense scrub and grasping thorn bushes creating an impenetrable barrier relieved only by the occasional outcrop of flat-topped acacias standing above the undergrowth. The semi-arid thicket covers many thousands of acres between the coastal plain and the western district in central Tanganyika and lies at a height of 950 to 1200 metres. The road between the capital Dar es Salaam on the Indian Ocean and inland Tabora stretches for over 460 miles or 740 kilometres, and the old slave route ran through it. Although officially forbidden in 1873 due to pressure from Britain, the slave trade continued for several more years.

The dusty track, hardly a road wound endlessly through the burning scrubland and I cannot recall ever meeting another vehicle there, though we had followed this route several times. It was like being on some inhospitable planet where Nature, springing from a barren soil, had produced a rare ugliness in this part of Africa. It was claustrophobic and slightly overwhelming. We dared not open the windows as it was tsetse fly country and the car grew hotter and more unbearable until we were forced to stop for a drink and to wipe our faces with a wet flannel from the cool box. The four of us were suffering from a lack of air and my husband Tom at the wheel, looked paler than usual; young Francesca's bright chat had quietened, her fair hair dark and damp with perspiration and sleeping Julian, thumb in mouth looked almost feverish. It was sweltering. Airless. Mid-afternoon, the hottest part of the day and we had been travelling since early morning. We came to a halt in a flurry of choking dust and within seconds hundreds of tsetse flies came crowding at the windows, buzzing and hitting the panes as they tried to get at us, alarming the children. I reached for the cool box saying, "Let's go it's awful here, I can get the drinks while we drive."

And then I saw them.

"rare, long-stemmed, speckled gigantic flower"

At first I thought they were the tall trunks of acacia trees with unusual markings then I realised I was looking at four long speckled legs close by the car. They seemed to go on forever and when I craned my neck I could see a pale furry tummy and then a long neck and found myself looking into the dark eyes of a giraffe that was peering down at me with equal interest. Gradually we were aware of many more of them, standing close together and appearing to be intrigued by the parked car and possibly the occupants since I imagine it was unusual for any traveller to choose to stop in this unforgiving and relentlessly hot part of the world

"Giraffes!" I breathed hardly daring to speak, hushing the children as they clambered onto our laps, Julian now awake.

"Look! Look! Lots of them," my voice quivering with excitement and awe as we spied another of the elegant shapes, then another and another. We were surrounded by a herd of giraffes, their hides beautifully marked with tan and russet and white jigsaw puzzle shapes, the tiny tufts on their heads covered in velvet, ears flicking and twitching as they investigated us with their gentle eyes. There must have been eight or ten of them not all the same height or age; some looked like teenagers with paler coats and lighter bodies. The mature animals' heads were level with the tops of the acacia trees — several straddled their front legs slightly as if to observe us, swaying their graceful necks from side to side as they bent down moving closer to our car with obvious interest; they were unafraid.

For a while, how long I have no idea we regarded one another in silence. They appeared to be simply intrigued then as if on a command they all turned — they'd seen enough and moved slowly off, their ungainly legs moving in unison, heads swaying like flowers in the wind. Later, much later I read Karen Blixen's description of a herd of giraffes; she felt they were unlike a herd of animals but also likened them to unusual dappled swaying flowers. To that description I would add one word. Exotic.

All of a sudden they were gone and we were left with the thicket, the dry acacias and the buzzing of tsetse fly in the middle of the African bush.

CHAPTER EIGHT

THE SWIMMING POOL
Windmills and gardening

Packets of pale blue tiles lined the surrounds of the hole in the ground one morning when we returned from the market — this must mean that Mikalis had managed to get hold of a tiler and would be about to begin. Perhaps the pool would be finished before the end of summer? We were quite excited for a few days but nothing happened, so with our newly learned Cretan philosophy we forgot about it and thought of other things. *Σιγά σιγά,* siga-siga, slowly-slowly, had of necessity become our motto. Mikalis became decidedly grumpy — his eyebrows meeting in the middle in a strong black line — so we kept our distance. His usually cheery *kalimera,* good day or good morning was barely audible and he didn't stop to talk on his way up the terraces. I even thought I heard the unmentionable word that begins with 'm' when a friend called in for a chat. It is a word not to be used in polite circles, I have been told.

One white-hot morning I noticed him checking the tiles and muttering to himself; then he sat on the garden wall beneath the loquat tree, his broad shoulders noticeably sagging. He seemed to be waiting for something — someone — a tiler perhaps? Everything seemed to be waiting; the pool that had been primed for tiling by Mikalis weeks earlier and it was now mid-August; we were waiting for a swim; the kittens too were waiting in the shade though not for a swim but for food which Mikalis had not given them on arrival. I joined him on the hot wall and asked him why he was cross. Was he ill? He rattled away in Greek — no he was not ill in the body he said, but his head was ill because the *ανθρώποι,* anthropi, men, who said they would come to work on the pool did not arrive; other *μαστόροι,* maestori, artisans, including *some* distant relative who was expert in pool tiling but was too rich and too lazy to work in the summer. They all said it was too hot even though he had offered more money than anyone else they refused to work in August. Wait for the winter, they laughed. They were all too rich, he said. He was quite distraught and I sensed a wave of very deep anger within and a continual frustration that was no doubt responsible for his many aches and pains; he was so often tense.

"*Isos avrio.*" Perhaps tomorrow he said and he was not going to wait any longer. I watched him stump down the terraces scattering kittens as he went and when he drove off in his little blue van he accelerated like a madman and the vehicle almost left the road; back to Agios Nikolaos where he would undoubtedly be venting his spleen on his poor long-suffering family.

At eight o'clock the next morning we heard voices drifting up from the lower terrace. Could this mean the tilers were here? We went to investigate and Mikalis introduced us to someone called 'Manoli" who was not exactly prepossessing to look at; a short barrel-chested man with spindly legs, wild matted hair and a wayward eye, cigarette dangling from his lips and it didn't take us long to realise that he seldom, if ever, washed. His expertise, according to Mikalis, was in the throwing on of cement, roughing up the surface to accept a coat of whitewash that gave the Mediterranean stucco effect. First, he threw it forcefully at the sides of the pool, then the surrounding parapet and over the crude drystone walls throughout the terraced gardens. It was not an amicable relationship however and the ensuing Greek dramas and shouting matches between the two men ended with Manolis charging off the property shouting obscenities, never to be seen again with the pool incomplete, but well on the way

Time passed and work continued with Mikalis and a surprising collection of helpers – tilers they were not! Three exceedingly small men with pale curly hair, the sort of hair that might indicate a vitamin deficiency often seen amongst indigenous people who have been raised on inadequate diets. Their figures were barrel-chested with short legs, stunted. They lit three cigarettes and hovered over the vast hole in the ground – now mostly tiled –and chattered in muted voices amongst themselves. Julian and I looked at one another; perhaps they were relations.

"No," my son replied confidently. Mikalis will probably be along any minute."

As he spoke the trio jumped into the pool and began to argue excitedly with each other; one of them was evidently in charge and with the help of one of Mikalis' rickety chairs, climbed out and began handing down the tiles; another followed him and seemed to be searching for something, shouting and gesticulating wildly; then they both jumped down and sat cross-legged in the middle of the pool — where I suspect the temperature was well over forty degrees — and lit another cigarette. Having rested and smoked, they climbed out of the pool and trudged up the path to the top terrace behind the future Villa Seven where Mikalis stored everything including several forty-four-gallon drums of ασβέστης, asvestis, asbestos, a lime mortar that when mixed with an element transported from the volcanic island of Santorini makes a true cement or plaster. The material arrives from Santorini in rock form with a chalky quality both in appearance and to the touch; Mikalis mixes it in huge drums with cold water that immediately begins to bubble and boil like a witch's cauldron that fills the air with clouds of acrid smelling steam. Very good for mosquitoes says Mikalis — or does he mean *bad* for mosquitoes? Initially great heat is generated as the rocks dissolve and after a day this gradually subsides leaving the drums full of a pasty substance a bit like melted butter or ghee. This has many uses:

— for whitewashing, a little olive oil and salt are added and the villa walls are rapidly restored to gleaming white with a long brush.

— for touching up dirty marks, no scrubbing to remove greasy spots, just slap on ασβέστης and in a couple of hours the surface is as good as new; it is also impermeable as one can wipe it down and the surface remains stable.

— for cementing, mix with cement and sifted sand and apply to surfaces; the mortar gives a creamy finish and is easy to apply.

— for stucco, a finer version of this mixture is used; this gives the rough finish typical of Mediterranean dwellings. As a bonus the cohesive force of the plaster has considerable structural value when applied to surfaces; the Minoans at Knossos and other palaces on Crete reputedly used this same mixture. It is as old as the hills and is recorded in history.

The little men returned with tins of *asvestis* which they mixed with fine sand that had been sifted earlier and once again used by the kittens and cats with delight. Once mixed it was slapped onto the sides of the pool and five tiles were put in place after another session of argument and dissent and boisterous childlike behaviour. Then they sat down again and had a cigarette as they surveyed the five tiles.

At that stage Mikalis arrived following a bus-driving stint that had made him later than usual. He greeted them with caution, his brows knotted and when he saw the five tiles he exploded with black rage; the air was thick with invective and the three men appeared to grow smaller as he approached with great strides and leapt into the pool with surprising agility for a man in his mid-fifties suffering from multiple muscular problems and — according to him — also crippling aches and pains. With one movement he ripped off the carefully placed tiles literally roaring at the astonished trio who were now huddled in the corner of the empty pool. We heard *that word* quite often and several other choice phrases and later over a glass of wine he told us that the tilers had laid the five tiles leaving no space for grouting.

Now any fool knows that one uses grouting between tiles, even I know that but apparently they did not. Conjecture ran wild in the family. If they didn't know the raw basics of tile-laying what sort of disasters could we expect when they reached the corners for instance or the circular indentations for the lights? We were somewhat gloomy until Mikalis assured us that he was taking time off from bus driving and would be at Villa Olga κάθε μέρα, kathe mera, every day from now on. We agreed this was imperative and the gloom lifted; Mikalis would keep an eye on things.

And he did! When he wasn't working with the trio he would sit under the loquat tree with his cotton hat on and glare down at them as they worked, eyes fierce beneath heavy brows. He interfered and interrupted incessantly until I began to feel sorry for them; but I noticed that immediately after he left for the town they stopped working, sat on the floor of the pool and smoked, slept and lazed around, leaping to their feet when they heard him return. Several times the smaller boss-man and his mate took off a few minutes following Mikalis' departure, with a screech of brakes and smoke as they did a U-turn on the mountain road below us, heading for Agios Nikolaos and undoubtedly the consolation of several shots of whiskey, a favourite tipple with Greeks, ouzo or raki, possibly all three? The remaining youth slept in the wheelbarrow at the bottom of the pool. On his return, Mikalis of course knew exactly what had been going on and seethed for hours muttering and stamping his feet more heavily than usual as he raged up and down the terraces.

On the third day the numbers increased to *four* little men 'working' on the pool; efficiency however, did not increase with numbers. Their thought processes — if indeed they had any — simply did not gel. They approached their tasks most laboriously; it never entered their heads to prepare the day's asbestos requirements first, place the tiles and necessary tools *in* the pool and then start to work. They did things in fits and starts or not at all and progress was very, very slow — not assisted I have to admit, by Mikalis' continued intervention. On about the sixth day we were surprised to find yet another small man in the pool. It was becoming somewhat crowded and if anything more inefficient than ever; more men meant less work and more noise and ribaldry. Two of them made eyes at Francesca much to her amusement followed by coarse language and nudge-nudge body language directed I am certain, at females in general. Their comments that mostly I could not understand fortunately, had that macho ring about them but it was nothing more than boyish flexing of muscles and a surge of testosterone, and it did not offend us.

A problem erupted with the paving of the pool surrounds by which time there were six men giving rise to our naming the entire project, 'Mikalis and the six little men'. Several weeks earlier I had shown Mikalis a picture in a glossy Greek holiday magazine with attractive mosaic paving around a pool and suggested we might do the same. He was impressed and agreed we should have *mosaiko,* like the picture. The stone he chose known as ironstone, is the hardest form of limestone and it comes in the colours of nature herself: silvery grey-green of the olives; russet-gold reflecting sunlight on the stone walls of Villa Olga; opalescent grey as found in the beach pebbles which when washed by the sea turn a deeper shade in perfect harmony with the dark taupe and honey tones of the wet sand. There is even a stone that reflects the blue-green shades of the carob and a pale, dove grey with attractive graining resembling petrified moss. All were chosen by the artist Mikalis.

The actual placing of the irregular flagstones was fraught with Greek drama for each time the men, and I cannot in all conscience call them 'tilers', placed them in Mikalis' absence, he would rip them up with a roar of absolute fury that echoed up and down the terraces and frightened the cats; they were either laid crookedly where they should be straight, or the wrong colours were side by side. One evening he roped in Yiannis and they removed the entire length of flagstones to be started again the next day. *He* and he alone would lay the paving around the pool — it would be slow but at least it would be πολύ ωραία, poli orea, very nice. Hope springs eternal!

*

And now, at the beginning of September just as the weather is cooling imperceptibly as though it knows summer is nearly over — the pool is filling. There were a few other problems such as the row he had with the man from Heraklion who fixed the pump in the newly-built storeroom beneath the pool. It was bought as new. The best and the most expensive said Mikalis, his chest swelling visibly when he told us but Julian tells me it is twice as large as it needs to be for the size of the pool. Something triggered off suspicion in the wily old man's head and he opened up the 'new' pump to discover it smelt of chlorine and chemicals and clearly was not new. He exploded and the man from Heraklion left in a hurry; his wrath scared even Yiannis who said he was not prepared to discuss the matter on the same evening, he would wait until the next day when Mikalis had enjoyed a good night's sleep. And what was the man from Heraklion's reply? He offered to guarantee the pump's working life for as long as Mikalis wanted — how many years did he want, he asked Mikalis who became a little chastened having got revved up for a major Greek drama. He asked us. Five we said. So the new pump, which was not new though the man from Heraklion never once admitted this, was guaranteed for five years and Mikalis was silenced.

Today he was blissfully happy, painting the attractive ironstone paving with a gloss that captured the depth of colour forever — as if perpetually washed by the waves. He wanted no one else to be involved in the finishing touches — like any artist completing his masterpiece, he was putting on the last few strokes. Water was trickling in from four hoses and all that remained was the arrival of the man from Heraklion to put in the chemicals and advise us how to maintain the pool. But would he come, we wondered or had Mikalis also scared him off for good?

We ventured to ask Mikalis how we would empty the pool when winter came? He told us that the outlet hose would empty the pool; it would run across the main road below the villas but we must ensure to empty it at night so no one knew what was happening, since the pool was illegal. Illegal? Somewhat aghast and with the innocence of the newcomer anxious to do the right thing in a true Anglo-Saxon manner, we checked with Yiannis. Yes, it was illegal he laughed.

"All the swimming pools they are illegal — everyone knows about it and nobody cares."

So that was that! 'We have to go with the flow' became our motto, it made life so much easier.

Last night the pool was half full and as a sickle moon rose in the sky and the evening cool descended Francesca ventured in, watched by us, Andrew, a visiting relative from San Francisco and by the Cretan family next door whose balcony overlooks the pool. Francesca pronounced the water to be warm and wonderful. Later, drinking wine on the balcony we raised a toast with clinking glasses calling στη πισίνα, stin pisina, to the pool — quite forgetting the six little men to whom we should now also raise our glasses. It does not leak. It looks fantastic and I cannot wait for a swim, and we all agreed a proper pool party was essential, we had to celebrate

*

Sitting on the waterfront one early evening at Elounda, we were marvelling at the soaring beauty of the bare taupe-coloured mountains behind the port when we spied several windmills high in the space of two hills. Seized with excitement we straddled our scooters and headed in the general direction of the windmills. The road wound through *Kato Elounda,* Lower Elounda, and *Pano Elounda,* Upper Elounda, both of which mercifully appeared to be quite untouched by progress. We negotiated our way through several hamlets perched on small hilltops surrounded by olive terraces; dilapidated cottages with tethered goats and dogs, chickens, donkeys laden with hay and the usual elderly Cretan women — slight and bent, many with fine features and light eyes — who scrutinised us with sharp curiosity. Few men, no young people, a feature of all the inland villages for the young have fled and the retired and grizzled males are to be found in the town *kafenia* drinking coffee and arguing about politics. In the daytime hours the villages belong to the old women.

Up and around the steep hillside flanked by dry fields, yellowing thistles and ancient olives with twisted trunks, each tiny plot is contained by grey stone walls. Far below the valley of Elounda stretched out into the sea with its surrounding arm of land enclosing the sheltered Bay of Spinalonga with the dun-coloured buildings and fortress of Spinalonga Island at the end of the arm. As we wound up higher the curiously rounded shapes of the barren massifs loomed close revealing falls of grey shale. Breath-takingly strong and wild. Magnificent. We followed the road around its crest to the other side away from the Bay of Elounda, away from the coast past steep valleys and ravines dissected by stone walls and ancient *kalderimia* that are cobblestone-paved trails built for hoofed traffic. These donkey paths follow the contours of the hills from the valley floor almost to the summit. On this protected flank of the ridge of hills, the vegetation held more moisture and there were fine stands of dark green carob; the olive trees were sturdier. A steep dirt track led to the windmills, four of them standing sentinel on the ridge overlooking Elounda on one side and the mountain village of Pines on the other.

To our delight one of the windmills was working; the sails whirled around urged on by the strong wind and as we approached, a good-looking man with pale blue eyes and fair skin hailed us. We introduced ourselves and he initially spoke in German until we told him we were English. He spoke a little English and told us he was Cretan and presented himself in a gentlemanly fashion — the suffix '*akis*' in his surname meaning 'little' is the clue to most Cretan surnames. This was imposed I gather, by the Turks during their four-hundred-year rule as a way of belittling the Cretans. He seemed almost excited to show us around his windmill as it creaked and groaned in the wind. Inside the small stone tower, we climbed perpendicular steps and found ourselves on a narrow platform where the corn was being fed between two great circular slabs of stone — the top one spinning around and crushing the corn that was then channelled through a narrow shaft to the ground floor where the now finely-ground flour was fed into hessian sacks. He showed us with pride how the main drive shaft could be slotted into wooden cogs to change the position of the sails when the wind altered direction. So simple and so effective. The mill was in fact only fifty years old though there had been windmills in this spot πάντα, panda, forever, he said. He told us that two of the mills were functioning; one had been converted into a house for tourists but was now deserted.

We walked across the stony path and peered in through a small window — nothing to see but a collapsed bedstead and a few things scattered on the dirt floor. We turned away and followed an overgrown flagstone path that led away from the windmill towards the edge of the saddle between the hills and found to our surprise, an empty bright blue kidney-shaped swimming pool with a million-dollar view of Elounda far below; garden lights lay broken on the ground and hundreds of broken bottles and empty beer cans littered the surrounds; evidence of some worthy pool parties on those heights.

The fourth mill had no sails and contained a fat sow with eight piglets grunting and snorting; their ears pricked up as they heard our voices. The stench was overpowering and we heard more grunting; just below the mill a stone enclosure held about twenty fully-grown pigs in filthy condition, but they were as fat as butter. Oversexed too for a slight exercise was in process as a young sow tried unsuccessfully to mount a recalcitrant young boar who wanted only to get as far away as possible. As she stood on her pointed hooves with her pink skin, albeit mud-caked, the curvaceous shape of her calf and thigh made her look for all the world like a naked woman in high-heeled shoes — positively human.

Standing up there in the slanting rays of the evening sun with the mountains turning mauve and the creaking rotating sails I could feel the centuries around me — the great age of this island. There had been windmills in that high and windy place for aeons, with corn being ground and taken to the villages by donkeys then bartered perhaps for *horta,* wild vegetables, or the many fruits that are common to Crete; the list is endless and includes all the citrus fruits, wild pear, prickly pear cactus, peaches, quince, apple, mulberry — the latter introduced for the silk trade and to be found in every village — and carob, olive and grape, all of which were grown in Crete during the Bronze Age.

*

The countryside is now dry and barren and on any outing into the hills one is assailed by the aromatic fragrance of the many herbs that grow profusely and are inadvertently crushed underfoot, releasing their bewitching pungency. We pick sage, thyme, marjoram, oregano and mint on our excursions and our pockets hold their aromas even after washing. In the window of every taverna and humble cottage there stands a pot of basil; it discourages flies they say and the village women often carry a sprig with them; it is not included in their diet though. We have been given masses of basil by the old women in Ellinika just above our villas, but they argued amongst themselves for a good five minutes on the best way to plant cuttings. This week, Nathalie is planting more herbs and vegetables for the winter on the narrow terrace alongside the property and if half the basil seeds come up we will be eating it forevermore. How hard she works, this fine, strong young woman. Our pot of miniature-leafed Greek basil has flavoured our omelettes, fresh tomatoes and vegetable concoctions for the past four months and is just keeping pace with our needs.

Gardening in Crete is a continual surprise and pleasure. I have created gardens in Tanganyika, Uganda, North Queensland, Canberra and grew pot plants on a balcony in Sydney but I have never seen such rapid growth springing from soil that looks like red clay and has seen no rain for five months. The soil is astonishingly productive; seedlings force their ways through the hard surface and in no time grow to mature flowering plants. Three months ago, I spread marigold and stock seeds on two new beds interspersed with geranium cuttings and already the borders are bright with pink and scarlet blooms and the pungent orange and brown marigolds are taking over with a vengeance. Nasturtium seeds planted only six weeks ago are miniature but already flowering yet when I planted them early September, I said to myself, "This is ridiculously late to plant nasturtiums, Valerie," but went ahead regardless. Now they reward me with their cheerful sunny faces even before they have matured. This week we planted a selection of bulbs in the certainty that spring will be magnificent if one can judge from the recorded winter temperatures that range from twelve to fifteen degrees between December and March.

Like most gardeners, I am shameless about helping myself to other people's seeds and cuttings and have returned recently with pockets of zinnia, sunflower and bachelor's button seeds from a few roadside plots, though I do draw the line at actually going *inside* someone else's property. I have sprinkled the seeds at random for I love wild, untamed gardens where nature continues to have her say. We all have a passion for growing things and to share this terraced garden with my family and with Mikalis — who keeps a sharp eye on everything we do and now, after a cautious start, approves our efforts — is a rewarding experience.

The eight terraces over which the villas sprawl, are planted with citrus and olive trees whose slender branches now hang heavy with tiny hard green olives that Mikalis tells me are the best for oil. The larger variety is reserved for eating. These trees are home to the cicadas which have disappeared entirely with the last heat of the summer sun— and I regret to say— due in some part to the kittens who on hearing their screech pricked up their outsize bat ears which they have yet to grow into, raced up the trees to return with a writhing cicada that as often as not would drop at our feet in the villa. They are half-wild, these Cretan kittens, for all our civilising influence and they hunt instinctively.

*

Tragedy has struck and we do not know whether it was the result of poisoned bait put out for rats — not by us — or a virus, but we almost lost two of our cats, Jupiter and Europa with a severe and paralysing illness. We took Jupiter by taxi to Agios Nikolaos to find a vet but he was away for a week on holiday so Francesca and I walked the length and breadth of the town asking people for advice. "Give him *lathi,"* oil, they said.

 So we took him back and dosed him liberally with pure olive oil — whether or not that did the trick we will never know, but he gradually improved and the paralysis left him. Then Europa was affected. She lost her balance and sight and it seemed as if she was suffering excruciating pain in her head for days. We three girls took turns nursing them both with tears in our eyes; throughout the cooler nights we refilled hot water bottles and kept waking the pair from their paralytic stupor to stimulate them while watching with sinking hearts as they failed to rally round. They were near death for so long, then little Persephone — to be called Titbits in later days — suffered a mild paralysis of the back quarters and had a hot dry nose for a day or so, but recovered quite rapidly.

I do not believe that our Australian-bred cats would have pulled through this episode which Mikalis assures us, was caused by poison from a man in the village who hates cats, particularly those belonging to Villa Olga. Perhaps there is more to this than meets the eye for Mikalis gets angry whenever he speaks of this man. These are Cretan cats — born to survive; slender creatures with long tails and necks, grey tabby stripes on white, huge ears moving more sensitively than those of other felines; more alert, possibly more intelligent or at least their instincts not dulled by over-cosseting and over-feeding. It is interesting to observe the closeness we developed during their illness has remained, particularly with Europa, who now shares my bed most nights. She purrs more, talks more. A loving cat.

CHAPTER NINE

EXPLORING THE ISLAND
Knossos — Palace of the Minoans

Autumn heralded a change of weather pattern so rapid that it took our breath away. One day we were swimming and sunning around the pool and in the bay though admittedly the days were shorter and the mornings and evenings much cooler, and the next we were shivering in our thin slacks and t-shirts, searching our cases for socks; the cats were finding the tiled floors too cold to sit on and were huddled together somewhat perplexed on the chairs and beds. Then the rain set in — and what rain! The vista of bay and mountains contracted as sweeps of sullen battleship grey clouds rolled across with sea and sky anchored to one another by slanting curtains of rain and yellow shafts of sunlight. Wind-blown cats' paws rippled across the surface of the sea as the bay heaved and rolled with a motion set up somewhere far away in the deep ocean. Thunder rolled around with crashing Wagnerian chords and lightning lit up the sky as mighty and marvellous storms enveloped us almost daily; they were accompanied by violent and capricious winds that whipped the fruit trees, shook off hundreds of olives and flattened nasturtiums and marigolds. The steep terraces ran with rivers of water and Mikalis phoned anxiously from town to see how and if, we were surviving. We inspected the villas for leaks and were relieved to find our badly fitting bathroom window was the only problem. Mikalis dismissed this with a disdainful wave of his hand when we pointed it out and said, "*Lógo tou Vóreiou anémou,*" which I gathered meant 'Due to the North wind' — implying there would be more to come. Hells bells. Mind you, I love storms so the bigger the better!

Yiannis had warned us that Studio Three would become uninhabitable if — and this was stressed — *if* it rained for three weeks which it hardly ever did, he said. I wondered about this. What if it rained for two and a half weeks — would the studio be only half habitable? He explained with a grin that the water ran down the back wall and out of the door. We watched the studio with eagle eyes through the initial spell of heavy rain but saw no sign of dampness — however it is not on the leasing list for this winter, not that anyone will come, we know that.

On the third day of drenching rain, we decided to try out the fireplace in Villa Two the largest and oldest of the villas which we all intended to move into for the winter. It was the most substantially built and had a spacious living room and open fireplace; a separate kitchen plus a half-bath in the bathroom. Positively luxurious. Julian and Nathalie spent the afternoon in raincoats bringing in damp wood, kindling and discarded planks while Francesca and I made a huge pot of vegetable soup; almost a stew which was deliciously satisfying with chunks of golden pumpkin, potatoes, carrots, a small turnip, onion, butter beans, celery and a bay leaf or two with herbs galore from the market. We tucked into this accompanied with delectable brown rolls fresh from the baker, having first lit the fire. It was a huge relief to find the chimney did not smoke; the wood crackled and spat furiously and the resin from the almond tree branches almost ignited before it touched the flames. The sitting room warmed up rapidly and we began to shed clothes and push the couch further back; how comforting it was to know that we would be warmed and cheered by an open fire throughout the forthcoming winter. The cats initially appeared nervous, what with the rain that they had not experienced in their short lifetime pelting down outside and the gutter from the flat roof overflowing noisily onto the balcony, plus the sharp crackling of the fire. Their sensitive ears twitched restlessly and they sat well away from the fireplace, close to us for protection. However, as the evening wore on, they approached the quieter embers and eventually sat on the rug, doing what cats do the world over — enjoying the man-made warmth.

The black and white television set which Mikalis said was out of order was simply not connected. Julian fiddled with some wires and we watched part of an American soapie in English with Greek subtitles, then a curious 'art' film from Finland with no sound. All in all, we decided music would be more rewarding. We talked of this and that, commenting every five minutes on the efficiency of the fireplace, the intensity of the heat and the fact that it didn't smoke. We found out later that when the wind was in a certain direction it did — and how — and we were sometimes forced to do without it and resort to the electric heater as the entire villa became filled with billowing eye-stinging clouds of smoke. But on our first really cold and wet night how cosy we were and what pleasure it gave us to light the fire and feel its warmth. The simple life. Absolute fulfilment.

*

Shopping became an interesting exercise as we attempted to predict the capricious weather and judge whether the break in the clouds meant that we could make a wild dash down the hill on our scooters. The problem was that the journey to the town square took ten minutes and the road wound down the sides of the steep hills on the edge of the bay, and at the junction of the main Heraklion and the Agios Nikolaos roads the wind came gusting through a break in the hills and when it rained, we were almost blinded. We tried wearing glasses and even swimming goggles but they didn't help at all; it felt like being inside a detergent-filled washing machine. The force of gusts through the gap in the hills practically blew us off our scooters and we often had a problem keeping them upright.

We realised with this onslaught of winter, albeit a freak one — it was twenty years since the last early cold snap Mikalis told us when we complained — that the need to buy a car was paramount. We followed the usual pattern when wanting information; ask everyone we met then turn to Yiannis who was tireless in helping us in every possible way. The facts as he reported them to us were daunting. Anything mechanical or electrical in Greece was subject to colossal tax and the prices were prohibitive; an average second-hand family car which could be bought elsewhere in Europe for say, four thousand Australian dollars would, in Greece after tax, cost anything from upwards of eight thousand dollars. It was a depressing scenario that presented itself to us. We would have to think about it.

The cold snap lasted a week and just as I was becoming inured to it, the torrential icy rain and wind abated and I woke to a still, calm morning. I stood on the balcony to survey the newly washed world; the hill between us and Elounda had miraculously acquired a water-colour wash of faintest green, the sky above was blue and the clouds sitting on the Thripte range across the bay were flushed with the pink of dawn. These mountains hidden for days, sharply reappeared with a clarity of light and detail we had not seen in the summer and with clarity came proximity. It was as if I could lean out and touch the jagged spine and pick up the island of Psirá that hugs the Siteia coastline. To the south, the square white shapes of the houses in Agios Nikolaos jutting into the bay were outlined with astonishing clarity. Everything was so much close*r* now the air was free of moisture.

*

And then the swallows came. Swirling and curving through the sky over the hill for where it had been raining in Crete, it was snowing in Macedonia and farther north; it was time for the annual migration. Thousands of birds with their graceful split tail shapes were wheeling and calling across the wide gorge in front of the villas and I wished for someone to share this magical experience with me but the others were asleep in various villas and I did not want to wake them. And — as with many of my wishes — it was granted, for at that moment my youngest daughter Philippa called me from Australia and I shared it with her with an excited breathlessness that she understood. Now there are swallows everywhere, chirping and chittering and other birds are returning since the heat has left the island; sparrows dart amongst the olives enticing the cats to climb to dangerous heights, swaying alarmingly on the spindly branches. I watched three bright yellow canaries fly past in formation and a friendly robin, the first I have seen, has taken up residence nearby and I heard the funereal calling of crows yesterday — better suited to a damp, grey English lawn than to the olive and maize-hued landscape of Crete. One afternoon as I sat outside a tiny white church at the top of one of the hills overlooking Agios Nikolaos, two eagles hung lazily in the blue sky looking down at me, attracted perhaps by my jazzy red and blue outfit. It is good to have birds around us again for I have missed them; it looks as if Cretan birds spend the summers in cooler temperatures in the high country. In Australia, even in a busy Sydney suburb the trees are full of birds, mainly brightly-coloured parrots of all kinds, friendly magpies and the ubiquitous currawongs with their amber eyes and long, sighing calls, cackling kookaburras that wake before dawn. I missed them all because Villa Olga remains bird-song silent through the searing summer months.

Two weeks ago, the villagers of Ellinika tethered a sheep in the final stages of pregnancy on the terraced olive grove above our villas. Three goats normally inhabit those dry terraces, tied by short ropes to olive trees whose lower branches have been neatly trimmed. Even the higher branches are bare of leaves as they stand well on their hind legs and have a long reach, often using their front legs to pull the branches down. Highly intelligent creatures are goats and I feel they must be so bored walking round and round their restricted territory, day in and day out, night in and night out. I have named the three suitably;

Dame Edith Evans is black and tan with a long Plantagenet upper lip and imperious expression;

Trotsky is elderly, dirty white with a goatee beard and eyes that look as if they are behind granny glasses;

Yiati, which means 'Why' in Greek, is young and attractive and continues to question her fate with a plaintive bleat.

They are all female — even Trotsky — and they are milked each evening by the old woman in black with the beard to match, from the village. Further up the slope where we park our scooters, is Query — another inquisitive goat, also black and white with curving horns which she likes to use for scratching and for pretending to butt me when I get too familiar. She bleats whenever we drive past and encourages us to tickle her head which is covered in coarse black fur. Her spine is so thin it stands out like a dinosaur's. I think she must have a bad case of worms but she seems content and who are we to judge what is best for sheep and goats, cats and dogs or even humans in a way of life that is foreign to us? We who have only our narrow, safe lives as yardsticks whereas these people hail from centuries of tradition and conditioning that has enabled them to survive in an environment of hardship and poverty — until quite recently — and to be subjugated to waves of different foreign occupation. We would have perished I am certain, so it is no wonder they view the life of an animal differently to the way we do; they are merely useful as a source of food, as guard dogs and rat catchers — nothing more. Mikalis is different; a sensitive man who loves cats and all animals and is highly critical of the villagers whom he considers to be backward and uncivilised.

The ewe produced twins last night. Friends in the villa nearest Ellinika heard grunts and sighs — no humans attended — and in the morning we found two frisky lambs — one pure black and one white with kohl-rimmed eyes as huge as saucers — enchanting with their wobbly woolly legs and shiny hooves and already so naughty, dancing out of range of the ewe's short tether and driving her to noisy distraction. She has a rich and very loud bleat that invades the entire complex and hillside interrupting the calm of this normally tranquil place, so I tell our guests that we are after all living in rural Crete and this is one of its many charms. I don't add "get used to it" but I'd like to!

*

Villa Olga backs onto the hamlet of Ellinika where there was a second-century temple dedicated to Aphrodite and Ares. This became a 'border temple' in settlement of a dispute between Lato to the south and Olous to the north. The brochures and Blue Guide of Crete declare that nothing now remains; however, an archaeologist acquaintance of ours pointed out what he said were the remains of ancient walls at the edge of the hamlet built with tight-fitting stones and within the tiny rooms, broad strong arches. Creepers and wide-eyed cats sit on the crumbling walls but disappointingly the rest of the Ellinika is new and ugly but for the bright and carefully tended small gardens.

Five kilometres north of Villa Olga is the port of Elounda, its tiny harbour filled with brightly painted *caiques* and as one rounds the hill from Ellinika, the view over Elounda Bay is stunning; the long peninsula of Spinalonga swells out from its narrow neck, extending northwards and running parallel to the coast and the town, creating a virtual salt lake; salt was mined here in ancient times and the salt pans are still visible. The entrance to the open sea is almost blocked by the small island of Nysí Spinalonga with its dun-coloured Venetian fortress and Turkish buildings that for the first fifty years of the twentieth century were used to house lepers. A Draconian ruse to rid Crete of the last Turkish stronghold, it is said. They did eventually leave.

The best way to see Spinalonga is out of season since the tiny island is over-run by loud-hailing tour boats and tourists during the summer. One can hire a private *caique* from Manolis's Fish Taverna at Plaka, a tiny port and fishing settlement that was once used as the main supply centre for the island. The boat will return to pick you up at an agreed time. This we did and spent several hours wandering round the small island which remains heavily fortified on the seaward side. We picnicked on the rocks and snorkelled in the clear waters around the rocky headland where Julian discovered intriguing shards of pottery and what looked suspiciously like human bones. At this macabre find we stopped looking and concentrated on the Cretan red wine we had brought with us and took the little boat back to the shore at the agreed time. I felt uncomfortable on Spinalonga Island. For me it remained a place of horror and terrible suffering that still lingered around the darker spider-ridden corners and sad crumbling walls; even the fresh salty wind did little to dispel the ghosts of the lepers that hovered there. I am sure I heard wailing and moaning as our little boat chugged back to the mainland. I would not go to Spinalonga again.

*

The extensive Dorian ruins of *Lato Etera* lie inland across the saddle of twin peaks due west from Agios Nikolaos. In Dorian times, 1100 BC, Agios Nikolaos — known as *Lato Pros Kamara* — was the twin city and port to *Lato Etera*. The sighing of the wind, the deep high valley divided by walls of perfectly dressed large stone slabs and the broad flight of steps leading to a platform, an altar perhaps, tangibly conjured up the past. Fortunately, the summer crowds do not visit *Lato Etera* with the same sense of urgency as other sites, possibly because it is not Minoan — but it is a beautiful, spiritual place with seldom anyone there.

*

Erica, one of my young musician friends from Australia, whom I have always called "my daughter four" visited us in August and she joined Francesca and me for a trip to the tiny islet of Mochlos, a Minoan site where jewellery of exceptional beauty has been unearthed; it is now in the Agios Nikolaos museum. We flew along the magnificent coast road at great speed on our gallant scooters, the wind in our hair, passing one another with whoops of exuberance like three modern-day witches on motorised broomsticks curving around rocky headlands and up steep hillsides, our engines screaming at the strain; slowing down now and then to catch a glimpse of pale sandy bays and peppermint green shallows. We passed the Minoan village of Gornia that we planned to visit on our way home; through the tiny flower-filled village of Kavousi — we would also stop there on the way back — then up along the northern edge of the Thripte mountain range. Stopped at the taverna at Platanos that is attached to a tiny church to drink in the vista of Mirabello Bay, Agios Nikolaos in the far distance and the mountains beyond. We attempted to identify the cluster of buildings at Villa Olga but the summer haze had softened the view and by midday, the mountains had disappeared altogether.

On reaching the limestone quarry that glows in ghostly fashion from the other side of the bay, we skidded down the wide loose gravel surface to the tiny fishing port of Mochlos, sitting at the end of a broad sweep of the valley. It is a quiet and restful place with the now-familiar δωμάτιο για ενοικίαση signs advertising rent rooms with tavernas shaded by ubiquitous mulberries and tamarisks hugging the rocky coastline; a few Germans quaffing beer and eating Greek salads plus an unusual sight in Crete, half a dozen yachts bobbing about in the shallows. We were told they belonged to the American archaeologists who spent their summers digging at Mochlos and Psirá, a larger island to the north.

We had barely dismounted from our scooters when Erica threw off her shorts and was in the warm water swimming across the narrow channel that separated the island from the mainland. I followed her and we wandered around the ruins that were only partly excavated and allowed our imaginations to run riot. During the Bronze Age when the sea level was lower, it was almost certainly a peninsula forming a safe harbour for Minoan seafarers. There is something special about these ancient sites in Crete; the Minoans and Dorians knew where to build their towns, ports and cities, whether within towering mountain ranges with unimpaired views around them to withstand invasion from other tribes, not necessarily from an aesthetic point of view although their love of beauty was possibly also a consideration, or on perfectly positioned sloping hillsides overlooking the ocean, cradled by protective massifs. Their settlements were always in a commanding and secure position.

On our way back, to my consternation there was no βενζίνη, benzine, gasoline, in Mohlos — in fact, warned the man, not even on the main road for fifteen kilometres. My scooter chewed up fuel, and my heart was in my mouth on the long haul up to Platanos; the gauge showed empty but luck was with us and I free-wheeled crazily down the steep mountain road to the only petrol station in the area. And then home.

We had ridden ninety-five kilometres by the time we returned to Villa Olga and we were weary — but what better way to spend a day with our senses saturated by history and the beauty and colour of the landscape that surrounded us? The varying shades of taupe-to-mauve-to evening pink of the mountains; the indigo blue of the sea depths; the pale gold terraces of dry grass crisscrossed with neat stands of silver-grey olives, the dark patches of carob trees; the sharp green of the vines and deeper greens of rows of vegetables in the valleys falling away from the mountain slopes; villages dwarfed by Byzantine churches with their sentinel cypresses and in the midst of a vast olive grove and almost unseen, another white church with curving arches against the bluest skies. Francesca, ever-ready to take her stunningly original photographs kept stopping in a cloud of dust — strong legs akimbo — to record our journey.

*

On another occasion Francesca, Andrew and I took a bus to Siteia and then on to Kato Zakros which is approached by the wildest, most inhospitable barren hills that plunge straight into the ocean; a desolate moonscape with little vegetation. Suddenly the alarmingly winding road turns sharply downwards to the village of Kato Zakros and the archaeological site lying on the northeast slope of the hill. The curious word *Zakro — Kato* means 'Lower' — could be derived from *Zakarou* which was the name given to the Sea Peoples who invaded Palestine in the thirteenth century BC, and possibly settled in this south-eastern corner of Crete. Objects including three elephant tusks found in the ruins bear out the thesis that the palace's economy was by sea trade both with Egypt and Syria.

One can leave the bus on the main road a few kilometres before Kato Zakros and walk down the spectacular gorge known as the Ravine of the Dead which was carved by the river that used to flow into the Bay of Zakros. The walk takes an hour and resembles a miniature Samaria Gorge with its towering red cliffs pitted with caves that were used as tombs during the Minoan period. Despite its disturbing name, it is a pleasing gorge though subject to flash floods as are all gorges following storms. We came across a pair of ewes with skittish lambs that gambolled away as we approached and we spied a tiny owl perched high; many birds hovered between the towering cliffs above us. Our plan to spend the night in Kato Zakros failed; we were outnumbered by several German tourists who on seeing us making our way to the accommodation hurried past us and took the last remaining rooms from under our noses. Ah well, it takes all sorts!

Change of plan. We swam in the inviting clear waters of the bay, enjoyed a Greek salad and fresh fruit washed down by *retsina* in one of the tavernas then returned to Siteia on the afternoon bus. We spent the night in a dilapidated but once elegant Turkish mansion that sported a colossal bathroom with marble floor and brass taps, situated on the crest of the hill overlooking the port. Next day after a late start, we explored the commanding though crumbling Venetian fortress and wandered round the somewhat scruffy town. Siteia is relatively new, rebuilt by the Turks in 1870. The Venetians abandoned it in 1651 after which it was demolished, so it has no buildings of any note apart from the fortress, or any feeling of history unlike the other major ports of Chania or Rethymnon. It is the centre of the sultana raisin crop and the growing of hothouse vegetables and flowers that line the valleys. The annual Raisin Festival on the last day of August attracts thousands of people and I told myself we would come to one in the future. It was interesting to see sultana grapes drying in the sun along the roadside, collecting all the fumes and dust of the highway traffic. I now eat them with some trepidation knowing how and in what manner they are dried.

Following delicious *souvlaki* and Greek salad by the harbour that unfortunately stank of sewage, not uncommon in these Cretan ports, we boarded the sleek *Ierapetra* inter-island ferry for a delightful two-and-a-half-hour trip to Agios Nikolaos and home to our comfortable villas. These ferries run frequently between the ports and are a cheap and enjoyable mode of travel.

*

The Minoan palace at Malia is half an hour's ride from Villa Olga just off the main road towards Heraklion; it was November and the site was deserted when a friend and I visited it one morning so we squeezed through the gate and walked around in silence, absorbing the feel of the place. Reconstruction has been kept to the minimum and the walls are not high but it is nevertheless imposing; the sea just visible. The ancient city was a major port and the bricks were made of an unusual combination of seaweed and clay. Several giant *pithoi,* clay pots, beautifully decorated and used for oil and grain storage stand alone while others surround the main central court. Common to all Minoan palaces the remains of huge columns rise in isolation.

•

When we visited the Minoan Palace at Knossos it had been raining heavily and the grounds were partly flooded with the lower chambers awash and the dark pines heavy with moisture scenting the cold air with their pungent aroma. In the absence of the summer crowds, I saw several areas I had missed on previous visits; the terracotta water pipes dating back to 2000BC were there and just beneath my feet under a metal grill, and I could more closely investigate the mighty frescoes in situ with their glowing reds, blues and yellows. The ungainly pillars that were originally the trunks of giant cypresses that used to cover the island were placed upside-down — hence the thickness at the top instead of the bottom to strongly support the storeys above. Knossos was several storeys high. As I stood there, stunned by the presence of the past, I realised that my question to Mrs Zimmerman all those years ago had finally been answered. It is difficult if not impossible for the layman to visualise what these ruins looked like thousands of years earlier so for me, Knossos with its partial restoration by Sir Arthur Evans is the best thing that could have happened. Archaeologists and purists argue and historians rant and rave about the damage his Draconian method of excavation wrought, but for the ordinary person the restorations — even if only partially accurate — do at least give one an *idea* of the architecture of the period, the colours of the frescos and finally the vastness of the palace grounds that cover over four acres. Arthur Evans estimated that the population could have been as high as eighty thousand at its peak though it is believed this figure is seriously exaggerated. The Archaeological Museum in Heraklion, four kilometres west of the Palace of Knossos is a *must*, and in my opinion, should be visited before going to the actual palace itself. The colours of the original frescoes — those at the palace are copies — on the upper level are amazingly fresh and bright.

Minoan pottery evolved through many stages yet retained its delicate depiction of nature; concentrating on flowers, animals and birds, plant life and marine creatures and of course the supremely beautiful human body as they saw it. Whether or not the Minoans were as lithe and slender as portrayed is not known; that they adorned themselves with exquisite jewellery and ornaments is unquestionable. It seems to have been a gentle and non-belligerent culture — no weapons of war have been found and their initial preference for building on the coast instead of hiding in the mountains, which they did later when invaders arrived on the island suggests that they were under no threat from assailants for many centuries. Something of this has rubbed off on today's Cretans. Although their island has been invaded and fought over, they have suffered extraordinary hardships — not least of which during the last war when the island was occupied by the Germans for four years. German words like *kaput* remain in the language; it means 'broken' or something unsuccessful. Cretans are a happy and gentle race but for the mountain people of Sfakia in western Crete where vendettas remain common. Hospitality abounds even at the end of the summer season when one would think they would have had their fill of visitors, but that is not the case, one is invited into their tiny dwellings in remote hamlets and given strong sweet coffee and shown where they tread their grapes; where they distil *raki*,the Cretan firewater similar to Italian *grappa* made from grape skins and stalks following the first pressing. Fruit and nuts are brought out and a small celebration develops within seconds with curious *yia-yias* in black arriving to investigate the presence of *xenia,* foreigners who traditionally are always welcome. This is a rewarding place to live.

Santorini – Afternoon – Thera '90

Villa Olga Summer '91

Santorini steamy afternoon

Villa Olga garden in summer

Monastery - Pyrgos
Santorini
VH

Santorini Monastery Profitis Elias

Crete, Chania backstreets

Geraniums

Helps

Dawn ʻSuvapaʼ – first rains
1989

First rains for ʻEuropaʼ the cat

The shepherd with pale eyes

A phantom schooner Mirabello Bay

View of Agios Nikolaos from Villa Six

Crete – Ἀγίος Νικόλαος Hazy dawn midsummer '92

Agios Nikolaos hazy dawn midsummer

Crete -- Spinalonpa-Island 1989

Spinalonga Island

Reconstructed shield frescoes from the Upper Hall of the Colonnades at Knossos 1991

Knossos from the Upper Hall of the Colonnades

Crete - Istron beach May 90

Istron Beach shimmering waters

first snow Nov '95 Dikte Mountains

Crete

Dikte mountains first snow

Venice, city of gondoliers

Agios Pandemelion Crete
1992
H

lelps

Agios Pandemelion

CHAPTER TEN

CHRISTMAS IN CRETE
The Lassithi Plateau and everyone has a car!

It was great seeing Penny again. The last time we met we were both ageing fast and incredibly stressed, eating a hurried sandwich in the park adjoining the Sydney Opera House that faces the sparkling harbour with its fussy ferry boats, yachts and other craft, and by our feet a squabble of ravenous seagulls. I miss Sydney Harbour though would not exchange it for my peaceful Mirabello Bay, ever-changing in mood and tone with its occasional sleek inter-island ferry boat and bright *caiques* like toys on a pond far beneath the slopes of Villa Olga. At the time Penny was running the Sydney International Piano Competition and I was the orchestra manager of the Opera and Ballet Orchestra then known as The Elizabethan Theatre Trust Orchestra with my office in the Sydney Opera House; both rewarding if exhausting careers.

That was early in the year and now in November of the same year I was in Crete and already established in the running of Villa Olga with its six villas with my son and his wife, my eldest daughter Francesca had just returned to Sydney vowing to come back as soon as she could, sadly her six months' leave had come to an end; and Penny had been in Peru for a stint on an archaeological site, working as a cook and was spending a week with me. before returning to Sydney. She was thinner and more worn than she had been at our last meeting from the challenging demands of the previous few months but — as always — full of enthusiasm to explore Crete. She hired a small car as we were still on our scooters and we set out on a three-day trip to my favourite places. The Lassithi Plateau was first on our list.

*

We drove westwards towards Heraklion for half an hour past the ancient site of Malia then turned inland to the massive Dikte mountain range, through the fertile basin and village of Mohlos and then wound upwards towards the sunken plains of Lassithi, hiding in the heights of the Cretan uplands. As we drove, the temperature dropped dramatically as the land fell steeply away from the mountain road into deep ravines and gorges. We were watched from on high by half a dozen bald-headed vultures and twice as many black ravens as they drifted around on air currents above a kill far below on the barren slopes. In the tiny village of Krasi, a pretty spot where a gushing spring leaps out from a Venetian stone water trough we found what is reputedly the largest and oldest plane tree in Crete. Its girth is reputedly that of twelve men with their arms outstretched and linked. Just beyond in the next village of Kerra one can see the spire-like peak of Karphi, standing 1150 metres above sea level. On its heights, a sanctuary and tombs were unearthed indicating that after the collapse of the Minoan civilisation the inhabitants fled to mountaintop eyries where they could better defend themselves. A dozen or so old corn mills stand sentry against the skyline at Seli Ambelou Pass; the natural gap between the soaring mountains on the western side of the plateau. As one drives through the view of the high plain is stunningly beautiful, even when the windmills are not fluttering 'like thousands of butterflies' as they used to. In any case no irrigation is needed when it rains almost every day in November; the windmill season lasts from May to October. Currently there are approximately three thousand windmills in working order — ten years ago there were ten thousand. Sadly, modern pumps are taking over and the old mills stand somewhat forlornly their sails rotting; at the current rate of progress, few of these picturesque windmills initiated by the Venetians in the fifteenth century — though these standing are only a hundred years old — will remain in the next century.

The Lassithi Plateau lies at an elevation of 866 metres encircled by the arms of the Dikte Mountains with peaks of over two thousand metres in height. This natural catchment area is the most productive land in Crete and has been cultivated for thousands of years. Excavations show that the plateau was inhabited during the Late Neolithic period 5000 BC and was densely populated in antiquity. Now only ten sparsely populated villages remain, scattered around the perimeter of the plain on higher ground to escape spring flooding. The plateau is too high for olive growing; however every inch of the land is cultivated and irrigated by windmills. Wheat has been grown since the seventeenth century and an abundance of potatoes and other grain crops is also produced on the plateau.

Looking down from the road the plain resembles a gorgeous patchwork quilt with stitched bottle-green hedges, furrowed and portioned fields of late cabbages and early winter vegetables; rich dark brown fields of newly ploughed land with autumn-tinged fruit trees laden with fruit — the ground beneath bright with windfalls; apples, quinces and pears in such abundance that we could not bear to see them go to waste so we picked until we could pick no more and on our return to Villa Olga we stewed and froze and ate fruit till we grew weary of the flavours.

For the moment, bearing in mind it is out of season, the Lassithi Plateau does not seem too disturbed by the twentieth century. A common sight is mules laden with produce ridden by old women in black– often led by elderly moustachioed Cretans in baggy trousers with high boots and round their heads the traditional, black, bobbled head-dress. Families till the fields; chickens and cats abound; tethered goats look up and bleat and there is an air of quiet contentment in this rural high valley; but winter is approaching and piles of firewood and kindling stacked high above the ground and pumpkins on the rooftops signal its approach. It snows heavily in Lassithi and outside the car the air was already sharp and biting.

Mikalis told us a story with great glee of a week spent in Lassithi last winter when his bus was snow-bound in four feet of snow; he drank village wine and no doubt other restorative substances and relaxed with his friends while Marika telephoned him daily, frantically worried about his health and welfare. A woman's role the world over.

On the western slopes of the plateau lie the village of Psychro and the Diktean cave, allegedly the birthplace — or rearing place depending on which book you read — of the god Zeus. The nasty story goes that Kronos, Rhea's husband, ate all his newborn children for fear of being unseated by them as had been predicted. Rhea, determined to save the infant Zeus gave birth while helpers danced and shouted to hide the child's cries and she gave Kronos a stone to swallow instead of the infant; this event is also believed to have occurred on Mount Ida. In any case, hundreds of objects of great beauty and mystical value — many of which can be seen in the Heraklion Museum — were found set into the stalactites in the vast limestone cave that is over seventy metres in depth. A shrine and a stagnant pool lie at the bottom of the cave which is rather dull and certainly not the interesting place I was expecting. We took a torch and climbed down the steep sides of the dank cavern, holding onto a rope that was necessary since the uneven steps were slippery with candle wax and damp; the descent was extremely slow and I was relieved to find we were the only visitors as I could imagine how unpleasant it would be if crowded in by hordes of tourists. The only lighting in the cave was from our torch though candles can be purchased at the mouth of the cave.

The streets of the little villages were grey and hazy, softened with smoke through which the rich autumn leaves of the various fruit trees glowed making a charming picture and when we ventured into a taverna in Tzermiado, the largest village on the northern side of Lassithi we discovered where the smoke came from. Each shop and taverna had a wood-burning stove around which everyone was gathered and from it, a pipe followed the ceiling and out through a hole in the wall into the street. Efficient but not quite like any chimney I have ever seen. We found a taverna with a welcoming wood stove and were greeted politely by rosy-cheeked Cretan farmers; they showed a friendly interest in these two middle-aged women travelling so late in the season. The owner spoke good English and was equally interested in finding us on the plateau in November and warned us to be careful of the snow that was forecast. Soon, he said. We sat at plastic-covered tables, warmed our frozen hands and feet and proceeded to enjoy a simple mouth-watering lunch; I am certain there is nothing quite as delicious on a cold day as Cretan *souvlakia* skewers of succulent herb-tasting grilled pork and a Greek salad topped with thick white slabs of feta cheese liberally doused with green olive oil sprinkled with oregano and the best chips in the world. Cretans par-boil their potatoes before plunging them into boiling pure olive oil and their flavour is unbeatable. We drank *retsina* in small thick glasses followed by Greek coffee which I gather is actually Turkish coffee, but it would not be wise to say so.

*

The hillsides above and around Tzermiado are heavily forested with huge holm oaks and maples that shone brightly in the afternoon sunshine as we visited Kroustallenia Montery, the religious centre of the plateau. It stands on a hillside with striking views of the plateau through trees and shrubs and within minutes, we were confronted by a miniature and shrivelled *yia-yia* in black who greeted us, said a rude word to the incessantly barking dog, then ushered us into the tiny chapel where she lit candles for us and chattered away completely unaware that I only caught one word in ten. Like many Greeks I met, she thought my knowledge of Greek was better than it was so I nodded brightly smiled and replied, *"Nai, nai,"* Yes, yes, at what seemed to be appropriate intervals.

No one has been able to establish the date or even the period when Kroustallenia was first built; it may have been as early as 1241; this view is based on a relief carving found in the sanctuary doorway of the church, but it is by no means certain that this carving always belonged to Kroustallenia. The inhabitants of the Lassithi Plateau have had more than their fair share of persecution from antiquity up to the present time. During Venetian rule, the plateau with its villages and churches and all its fruit trees was twice laid waste as punishment for some perceived outrage or other and its population was banned from living on Lassithi soil. Throughout the Turkish occupation, the plateau was under siege and thousands of Turks plundered and burned everything in sight, including the monastery in 1823. The Cretan revolution broke out in 1866 and the revolutionary committee installed itself in the monastery and once again paid dearly when Omar Pasha passed through. Rebuilt once more, the monastery was used by the Italians as a concentration camp during the German occupation; they encircled it with barbed wire and laid cement on the lovely grounds and later sent many of the prisoners to Nazi camps in Germany. It is hard to envisage the pain and suffering that the monastery has seen for there is such a sense of peace there — no spirits weep or sigh there now; perhaps the sheer beauty of the place has dispelled all memory of the violent past. The old buildings stand beneath shady trees and the paths are lined with gigantic hydrangeas with green flowers — the soil is evidently lacking in iron that is required for the usual blue flowers of the hydrangea. Our amiable *yia-yia* invited us into a communal kitchen and gave us cups of Greek coffee and on finding that Penny's name was Penelope — a Greek name — threw her skinny arms around my friend and hugged her with delight. She had been with the monastery for a long time for there were faded photographs on the rough walls of her standing with groups of wise-looking monks. I believe she said she had been there since she was a child but I am not sure I understood her correctly.

Crete has forty-two monastic communities and those that I have seen are without exception places of great beauty with gracious lines and façades built on commanding hilltops. I should like to visit them all. Monasteries by their very nature have always been centres of learning and wisdom and therefore power, and consequently a target for invading armies, particularly the Turks. In the Second World War, the Germans and Italians who paid scant respect to the monks and inhabitants of these sacred centres, commandeered them. The Germans twice arrested Abbot Ermolaos Kassapakis of Kroustallenia Monastery, who took to the hills to join the resistance fighters. I asked an educated Greek friend why it was that the Cretans still hated and in some instances still feared the Turks, but had apparently forgiven the Germans for the outrages they had inflicted more recently during the four-year occupation. He thought for a moment then said,

"Well. First of all, the Turks were here for four hundred years and the Germans only four years. Secondly, the Turks killed and destroyed entire communities just for the fun of it, whereas the Germans only acted in reprisal. And the reprisal *was* appalling. They warned the Resistance that if there were attacks on them there would be reprisals — but the Turks — they killed without reason."

That was his view and he was a thinking man; I also know that Mikalis has little love for the Germans, but being a realist does not mind their tourist Deutschmark.

*

We left the plain and wound slowly down through autumn colours and smoky hillsides to Mesa Potámi a mountain hamlet and stopped to investigate an interesting-looking pile of purple sludge on the roadside; an elderly man and his wife were distilling *raki* or *tsikoudia* in a tiny shack that was belching out smoke. The government permits grape growers to distil the second pressing of the grape and through many of the villages along the tortuous mountain road, the verges were stained with purple grape juice from the piles of skins and twigs waiting to be distilled.

We stopped to investigate and were invited into the small lean-to where a log was burning beneath a cylindrically shaped container full of the grape mixture. The man joined a second cylinder above it, sealing the join with mud and this gradually heated up and vaporised through a pipe running into another container sitting in a massive wooden barrel full of cold water. It finally condensed through an aperture to slowly drip into waiting bottles. We were given several miniature glasses to sample accompanied by peeled apples and pears — Cretans seldom drink without eating fruit and almonds from the great trees that grow profusely on the plain and the mountainsides. We sat on small rickety chairs and clinked glasses again and again with a cheery *stin yiamas*, to our/your health, enjoying the warmth and company of the fire for a while, not to mention the amazing effect of the raki coursing down our throats. It really *is* warming. Finally we pulled ourselves away from their overwhelming hospitality, and purchased half a sack of enormous potatoes, some walnuts, two bottles of village wine and several bottles of raki for Penny to take with her back to Australia. The slow and cautious drive home with barely any traffic en route while waving to other distillers was warm and relaxed — both driver and her passenger being very slightly intoxicated.

*

It was no longer a joke being car-less. We were supremely happy on our scooters until it began to get cold and once the shoulders of the day grew cooler and our faces, ears and hands froze, we started to look around for a vehicle. As mentioned previously, the price of any vehicle in Greece was exorbitant so we considered going to Italy where one of my three nieces who lives there, offered to help with our search for a cheaper car. The other option was to find a tax-free vehicle in Athens and hope that after six months we would be able to afford the mandatory tax which would be imposed. All sorts of schemes whirled around as the weather turned less friendly and became progressively more uncomfortable on the scooters; two of us developed earache and Mikalis insisted it was due to the change in the weather and us not having a car. He could be right. *Everyone* has a car, he frowned, brown eyes blazing, repeating the words ένα αυτοκίνητο, *ena aftokinito.* a car, time and time again. My unspoken reply referred to our dwindling bank account, the fact that it was off-season and that his villas were suitable only for summer occupation even though several had fireplaces, but my Greek was insufficiently developed for me to explain these unwholesome facts to this puzzled Cretan. *Everyone* had a car!

After a long search of a great many rust buckets since those were the only vehicles within our price range, Julian finally found a car with help from Cretan friends naturally enough. It was the nearest thing to a decent vehicle we could afford. She was a ten-year-old square-shaped Citroen Pony with canvas sides; ugly, draughty and bright yellow so I called her 'Buttercup'. Difficult to climb in and out of the back seats since there were only two doors and the front seats were fixed to the floor. There were also several defects that we discovered later when the windscreen wiper flew off in the middle of a rainstorm and on another occasion on the way to meet the plane at Heraklion the accelerator cable snapped. To add insult to injury there was no heating and winter was already upon us. Julian was able to invent an

145

efficient one but the snag was — and little did he realise that he was unable to turn it off for the summer! Last but not least on one of our first exploratory trips up into the Dikte mountains we had a puncture. The tyre exploded with a loud bang, and Nathalie almost had a heart attack she said using her delightfully French expressions, blue eyes wide. Fortunately, the spare was in reasonable condition and she and Julian fixed the problem in double-quick time but later we had to buy three new tyres.

It turned out that Buttercup was reasonably reliable, cheap to run and surprisingly comfortable. She was also quite good off-road, having strong pulling power in low gear on the goat tracks and up the foothills of the mountains. Above all, we found the freedom to explore and use her generally as our workhorse.

Interestingly we discovered that our vehicle was unregistered and had probably never been through a police check, but as a foreigner in a country renowned for its desirable laissez-faire attitude to the law I was determined to be legitimate and legal, although I had already discovered that Greeks are independent thinkers and seem to get away with almost anything. When I tackled Yiannis he laughed and replied,

"There is nothing for you to do!"

He raised his eyebrows and showed the whites of his eyes. I could read his thoughts and I laughed with him.

"These foreigners, they know *nothing!* They just make more work for themselves and for us!" He grinned and patted my shoulder.

"How many cars you think are registered? How many you believe are having a police check?" Laughing.

I discussed this with Julian and we both agreed that for the moment we would let sleeping dogs lie and go with the flow. So, Buttercup was never registered nor checked nor thank god, did anyone ever ask for her non-existent papers. Initially, I was a little apprehensive driving on what still seemed like the wrong side of the road but found it remarkably simple as soon as I took the wheel. She was a *very* small car which was another plus for Buttercup and her drivers. Another hurdle was overcome; anyway it was mainly in my mind and not a real hurdle at all. Richard Bach — the brilliant author of *Jonathan Livingston Seagull* and my favourite guru — writes of his philosophy in *Illusions*, his gem of a book and the warning is:

Beware. If you insist on concentrating and believing in your limitations they will most certainly become yours!

And he is right. *We* set our limitations. We can do anything — well almost anything we have set our minds to unless beforehand we have placed doubts and limitations on our capabilities. For instance, I knew with absolute certainty at least four years ago, that I would soon be enjoying Christmas in Crete– and I announced my intention at a gathering of family and friends as we shared our Christmas luncheon at Uriarra Crossing a few miles outside Canberra. We were sitting on wooden benches beneath shady casuarinas, tall and breathlessly still on the burning summer's day. The stream was almost non-existent; a mere trickle amongst the stones, disappointing as we had planned to swim and shoot the small rapids on our lilos, but the drought had put paid to these plans. When I made my pronouncement, probably after some warm wine, I recall thinking,

'You're quite mad Valerie — where will you get the money for this dream of yours?'

At that time I was being paid a pittance for my part-time job as administrator of the Canberra Youth Orchestra that I loved and I was also supporting my two teenage girls. I was struggling, but the dream was there. Eventually, the small house was sold, the takings shared with my ex-husband and I moved to Sydney to work with another youth orchestra, then to the Sydney Opera House for a few years and finally — to Crete. Simple as that and all laid out in front of me. It seems now, looking back on it that I didn't have much to do with the events — they just happened as I knew they would. In this case, I did not argue my limitations but gave them free rein and here I am and what's more so are two of my children, which is more than I bargained for. A bonus indeed to share this adventure with them.

CHAPTER ELEVEN

WE HARVEST OLIVES
New Year's Day

On the fifth of December my twenty-two-year-old 'baby' Philippa and her boyfriend Paul arrived for a month's holiday; Francesca had left several months earlier for Sydney, vowing that she would return as soon as she could save up enough money so it was wonderful to have another daughter with me over Christmas.

*

The colours of Crete metamorphose in December. The white pulsating light and blue shadows are replaced by a gentler shade of white — ivory perhaps — and the sky has clouds, a phenomenon not often experienced during the six months of summer. They alter the shape of the sky, bringing it closer and their shadows on the bay and the Thripte Mountains beyond softening the view from my villa. The island is transformed by the winter rain to a gentler, greener landscape, its harsh summer-brown outlines softened and rounded. The colours are kinder somehow, less strident than the summer and the air is finer, cooler though not cold with a promise of less heat; and suddenly there is dew in the mornings — moisture for the garden and the parched citrus and olive groves. A rest from the jubilance of summer.

For the Cretans and perhaps the Greeks in general, Christmas is not a time for exchanging gifts or undue celebration; traditionally this occurs on New Year's Eve when for the men, serious gambling takes place and entire olive groves, shops and businesses are lost and won, and just before midnight the gambling ceases and family affairs take precedence; cakes and sickly sweets are offered and gifts are given, but only to children up to the age of twelve.

Yiannis tells me that Greek Orthodox Easter usually falls on a different date to the Christian Easter and it is the highlight of the year; Christmas is really low key, left to the ex-patriots. Having said this, the little port of Agios Nikolaos now reverted to its small indigenous population following the summer invasion, was looking somewhat festive with synthetic trees, tinsel, glittering sleighs and cribs hanging between the trees. The more up-market shops of which there are still mercifully few, sell baubles and decorations and Greek Christmas cards are either quite charming — copies of Venetian tapestries with galleons, historic scenes in rich colours, gaudy flowers and sad-eyed saints robed in gold and purple — or awful — Woollie's worst with badly drawn Christmas scenes of anaemic robins and pallid children in the snow.

I was sadly disappointed with the Englishness of it all. Tourism had a lot to answer for and many ex-patriots were living permanently in the area and they too had changed the face of the little harbour town. Invasive loudspeakers broadcast English carols and a few Greek songs; all the oldies were churned out and the streets reverberated with the velvety tones of Bing Crosby's 'White Christmas' and an indifferent rendition of 'Jingle Bells.'

In a Cretan fishing port, these sounds were inappropriate and began to pall and finally to irritate to the point of desperation so I sought out the man responsible for the Christmas music — he owned a leather shop on the edge of the square and his daughter learnt music at the local School of Music. He said it was a thankless task. The locals complained that the music was too loud, too soft, not enough Greek tunes, too many English carols. He would not do it again for the council next year, he assured me. I fervently hoped that no one would take on the job.

*

Crete being a long, slender island is subject to frequent changes in weather throughout the year and it has kept us on our toes. In December the average temperature was pleasant with the thermometer hovering in the early twenties, though there would be a thick cover of snow on the Dikte Mountains and the icy cold gusts were biting. Throughout the year a wild wind could appear from nowhere, either from *Vóreios*, the north or the Libyan *sirókos*, sirocco — hot and sand-laden that came sweeping through the gap in the mountains to the south churning the bay into a frenzy and leaving a thick layer of yellow desert sand on every surface.

"Próvlima." Problem, Mikalis would say, his heavy eyebrows lifting upwards, anxious about the young citrus blossom and the wind.

"Megálo próvlima." Big problem — in his thick Cretan dialect that I found so hard to understand.

*

On Christmas Eve we persuaded Philippa to play her violin for us; reluctant she was but after supper as we lolled in front of the fire, she took her instrument out of its case and dressed in a baggy tracksuit and jumper, blonde hair silky and straight to her shoulders, she began to play the *Adagio* from Wieniawski's Second Violin Concerto, one of her favourite pieces. I have always been amazed at the volume of sound that my daughter can coax from her violin; her small frame seems to be taken over by some inner strength as passion and perfection soar out as she enters another world, absorbed and consumed by the music. We sat transfixed and deeply moved by her mastery of the instrument and I noticed that we all had tears in our eyes when she finished playing. I for one continued to marvel at the dexterity and control of my youngest daughter who has always been too lazy to practice.

Christmas Day dawned bright and sunny, but as Mikalis and family arrived laden with cakes and biscuits, bottles of wine and liqueurs, clouds covered the sun and the rain began. This would have been alright but we were cooking a large piece of pork on an outside spit that Julian and Paul had taken hours to devise. It was a sturdy affair built with corrugated iron sides supported by bricks and it stood in the little courtyard off the kitchen behind our villa; the olive logs had already established glowing red coals when the rain came down. It poured. Hurriedly and with Mikalis' help, the boys erected a canopy of heavy plastic which only partially covered the spit and we took turns sitting in our raincoats beneath an umbrella — rotating the handle, the hot fat sizzling and protesting as the rain thundered down. We also had a sizeable turkey that we had stuffed; Villa Two had an electric stove with an oven — unlike the other villas that had only gas burners — but it was ancient with rust-encrusted sides that allowed most of the heat to escape so the temperature never became hot enough to seal the turkey juices. In the courtyard Mikalis had built a traditional Cretan oven which was a large clay pot turned on its side with another pot as a chimney, so we placed the stuffed bird in the outside oven that was glowing with heat for half an hour, then transferred it back to the old stove in the kitchen. We roasted the potatoes, onions and pumpkin in the outside oven — dashing in and out of the pelting rain in our raincoats, balancing trays of food. Somehow we managed to cook everything, shored up by several glasses of explosive raki and had it all ready at the same time — how I will never know. Succulent turkey, aromatic with herbs and delectable stuffing and crunchy pork surrounded by roast vegetables and crisp potatoes; a triumphant meal, complete with crackers and daft party hats from France.

Naturally enough we had been unable to find Christmas puddings or mincemeat in the shops; anyway I felt we should have a Cretan Christmas, not realising they do not consider it anything special. However they do bake wonderful pastries including *Christopsomo,* Christmas bread that is yeasty though in my opinion, is a rather tasteless loaf of gigantic proportions filled with figs and sultanas. The word means Christ's bread and the loaf is decorated with a cross.

Marika's contributions began arriving several days earlier to complete our Anglo-Cretan Christmas dinner; she and her daughter Olga had been cooking for days in their flat in Agios Nikolaos and they brought the most amazing selection of sweet pastries including *kourampiédes, c*rescent-shaped almond shortbread drenched with icing sugar; *melomakárona,* honey cakes with semolina; *loukoumades,* sweet and feathery honey puffs with sesame seeds introduced by the Phoenicians centuries ago; and of course *baklava,* oozing honey lemon and crushed walnuts and yet another soft biscuit, peppery with ginger; a plethora of Cretan riches from heaven — so delicious that words failed me. Our purchased rum balls, chocolate and walnut mounds and pink and white sugared almonds paled to insignificance beside Marika's fabulous artistry and the way she and Olga arranged their pastries on platters and trays was impressive. None of us wanted to disturb their carefully arranged works of art. We barely knew where to begin.

We were ten at the table; Mikalis and his wife Marika, Yiannis and Olga; Philippa and Paul; Julian and Nathalie and her mother Danielle on a visit from France and me. We drank various wines including a delicious rosé and the villa resonated with our bright toasts to all and sundry as the evening wore on. Following the meal I made Turkish coffee by filling a tiny long-handled *vriki,* traditional coffee pot with water, loads of sugar and finely ground coffee beans, boiled it up three times then poured the frothing syrup into tiny white cups with glasses of iced water.

Hours later we left the table satiated and sat like exhausted rag dolls stunned by good living in front of the fire that Mikalis had insisted on lighting, though the day was not cold. He insisted a fire added 'another friend' to our group and he was right of course; a fire does have a life and voice of its own. Neither Marika nor Mikalis spoke any English but our communication was unimpaired since Olga and Yiannis were bilingual and we were friends; body language helped a great deal. The villa, the crackling fire, the abundance of food and wine and phone calls brought the rest of my family closer and were sufficient to make our first Christmas in Crete truly memorable.

Before our guests departed we wandered around the glistening terraces together; the rain had abated and the garden was washed clean with the sun on the bay giving it back its blue tones. The leaves on the grapevines and apricot trees were turning and the pistachios above the pool now bare of leaves, their pale trunks stark against the stuccoed walls; the many citrus trees bending with ripening golden oranges and sharp yellow lemons and tiny mandarins stood knee-deep in the yellow oxalis that covered the island. The heavy scent of orange blossom, white and waxy filled the air and the garden was full of birds foraging for worms while my russet-breasted robin hopped around on spindly legs attracting the attention of our sharp-eared cats that drew back when I chastised them. The mountains across the bay stood out clear and sharp and close enough to reach out and stroke them. What rewards had come into our lives.

And that night — an indescribable intoxication — the sky festooned with stars and the angular and curved shapes of the constellations that reminded me of my father and how often through my young life in Africa we had spent together observing the heavens — arm in arm with no doubt a silent cat or two at our heels, wondering what we were doing. And here in Crete, sublime nights silent and so still where the moon seems to be forever full and floating in the heavens stealing the light from the stars or lying on her back, a slim sylphlike mere suggestion of a moon, but with a promise of things to come. A lovely ancient Greek saying of seafarers goes something like this:

If the moon is upright, the captain can lie down;
if the incomplete moon is lying on its back,
the captain stands to the helm.

And the days — often sunny with Helios the Sun-God in Greek mythology driving his chariot from east to west across the sky bringing light to the Earth and at the end of each day when the journey of the sun is complete, returning to his eastern palace in a golden cup, and when the sky frowns and the *tramontana,* the north wind, tears the clouds into shreds and howls across the terraces at Villa Olga shaking the citrus trees and blowing their blossoms into the now-empty swimming pool, I do not mind — it signals another season and my second year on the island.

*

Why is it that on New Year's Day many of us feel the need to review the past twelve months and, if we are past our prime — and I have never been sure exactly *what* age the prime is, since I don't believe I have reached mine yet — and why do we regret the passing of another year? The reasons are many, due perhaps to slight excesses the previous night leading to a certain remorse and a feeling of uncomfortable mortality the next morning or to the suspicion that there were too few highs during the past year and that the lows outweighed the highs. Mind you I don't think that New Year's Day is all that special — after all, if we were following the old Julian calendar it would not be New Year's Day anyhow. As for me, New Year's Day was a cheerful and promising event apart from the fact that I had just said goodbye to Philippa and Paul They were returning to Sydney and I would not see them for a year or until I paid a flying visit back to Australia, and that hurt.

We had to say two goodbyes; the first time we took them to the airport the wind and weather were so foul the plane did not arrive. Of course there was no prior notice of this until we got to the airport in Heraklion. Back we came to Villa Olga for an enforced and rather strained wait of a couple of days with them both worrying about getting back to Sydney, Paul to his job and Philippa to a concert in which she was due to play. However, looking beyond my inner weepy state I faced the coming year with my usual optimism; my glass is always half full not half empty. I was convinced that Villa Olga would attract masses of visitors and be a Success with a capital 'S' and I would be able to see my remaining two daughters in Sydney quite often, wouldn't I?

Looking back on the year I found myself surprised and not a little overwhelmed at the enormity of our undertaking over the past eight months; turning our backs on our careers, familiar surroundings, our language, friends and family and striking a blow for a different existence on the other side of the world. Had we made the right decision? I have to admit to spending a few restless hours at my usual worrying time — just after three in the morning — wondering if indeed the decision had been the right one. Summer and autumn had passed like a happy dream, carried along as we were on a high — filled with new sights sounds and flavours, hard physical work and the constant challenge of a language insufficiently learned. Many visitors and friends had been to stay and we had enjoyed endless hours of fun and laughter but I knew it would not always be like this. The novelty would wear off and then, would we be able to earn enough for the three of us? Now it was winter — albeit with a fairly pleasant and sunny climate — few visitors came predictably enough and consequently we had no income at all nor any prospects of any until the spring.

*

In December Nathalie started work in Agios Nikolaos as a nanny to two little girls and teacher of French to their Greek mother, who was herself a teacher. It was a job she enjoyed and for which she was well paid. Her contribution partially relieved the spectre of 'no income' but our capital continued to drain away. Payment of the lease tri-annually, accountant's fees, electricity, the car; printing of the brochures which, though done through Tom, a friend in England still cost a good deal, not to mention postage the world over; storage fees for our belongings still sitting in Sydney awaiting my five-year residency papers that had not come through. The list went on so we did the only thing possible; Julian and I would harvest olives.

Several weeks earlier we had watched Mikalis and his family harvest the many olive trees at Villa Olga; first carefully laying nets beneath the trees, then whacking the branches with sticks until all the olives were in the nets. Occasionally they used electrically driven poles run off a generator with strips of plastic on the rotating ends that shook the olives off the higher branches; having done this, the crop had to be sorted by hand, all twigs and small branches removed before the olives and leaves were poured into hessian sacks then taken to the processing plant. They were long and tiring days especially for Marika who looked quite exhausted as did Olga, both unaccustomed to so many hours of physical exertion. They stopped for lunch which they had brought with them and sat on the unfinished balcony of the new villa and resisted all my entreaties to have coffee with us. Stoically they returned the next day and the next and stayed until the last of the trees had been stripped, before sorting the twigs. Labour intensive it is. No wonder olive oil is so expensive and now Julian and I were going to harvest another stand of Mikalis' family trees with a share in the spoils, either in oil or cash from its sale.

*

We set out one cold and windy morning early in January with Buttercup laden to the hilt with rolls of netting, hessian sacks, the electric motor and the two poles, sticks for beating the branches and an axe for chopping wood plus our picnic supplies. Leaving the road behind we followed a rough track that wound its way through a valley flanked by steep hills heavily wooded with old olives. The twisted trunks stood in bright green oxalis with their startling yellow flowers, long-stalked, soft-petalled. Beautiful countryside; quiet but for the waking birds. We passed a familiar sight, an old woman riding side-saddle on a mule, black headscarf knee-length stockings and gumboots, skinny legs sticking out like stalks from her thin dress. She was carrying a plastic oil container and as she returned our greeting I remarked,

"She's probably bringing the fuel for someone's motor," and we laughed. It seemed to be so improbable.

Mikalis' grove meandered up a hill from the narrow valley; the trees at the top were stunted and not worthy of harvesting but the lower olives were heavy with the glossy black fruit. We pulled off the road and began to unpack the car. A man was waiting in a parked truck, strutting up and down, hands thrust deep in his pockets. An irritable man. As we laid the nets carefully overlapping them so as not to lose any of the crop we heard people arguing; the old woman had arrived on her mule and was handing the man the fuel container — he berated her angrily and they parted with ill-feeling, her shrill tones splitting the quiet as she returned on her mule down the road and he to his olives. She had ridden a good six kilometres from Limnes, the nearest village to bring him the fuel.

It was the sort of day that made me want to lie down on the thick carpet of clover with its bright flowers and compose a sonnet 'To a Cretan Olive Grove'. Around me on gnarled twisted trees redolent with history, smooth purple olives glistened beneath their silvery leaves and high up from one of the terraces, the varied notes of sheep bells like metallic wind chimes drifted down to us. On the other hand, we were there to work not to wax lyrical — and work we did but only after pursuading the generator to start for it complained and argued for a good ten minutes before Julian bullied it into life. We climbed into separate branches of one of the old trees that Mikalis tells us are a good two hundred years old if not more — and set to with the rotating poles. Olives flew in every direction, ready and ripe for picking and easy to dislodge.

The poles were long and heavy so we devised cunning ways of leaning them against branches to take their weight, or holding them against our rib cage for support while the plastic strips whirled round and ripped into the branches. At first it was fun, sitting high up in the green-grey foliage seeking out the ripe black olives with the day shining brightly around us, but after a few hours it became painful and then taxing indeed. Having cleared the upper branches, we stood on the ground to harvest the lower ones but this was more of a strain as one had to take the full weight of the pole with no support other than one's body. It took an hour and a half to harvest the first tree.

Once the crop was picked we dragged the nets heavy with the crop to a stone wall nearby and I stood on the lower level and began sorting out the twigs and branches while Julian tackled another tree. We had been warned that the processing plants have a machine that sucks up the contents of the sacks but it rejects twigs, so careful and painstaking sorting was essential. It was not an unpleasant task; I found it quite therapeutic initially, my gloved hands sliding through the leaves and fruit — its aroma oily and earthy — rather pleasing in fact.

We had several breaks for coffee, hot and strong and tasting of wood smoke and later in the afternoon we lunched on brown rolls, cheese, olives — naturally — and baked potatoes drizzled with olive oil — naturally — that we'd placed in the little fire Julian had built; they tasted curiously sweet against their charred skins, we finished off with fresh fruit and got back to work. Our exhaustion levels seemed to match each other's, though as the afternoon wore on I gave up and stoked the fire while Julian continued valiantly to work.

I made encouraging noises like,

"Time for coffee?" or

"The next lot of potatoes must be ready by now surely?"

Eventually he too gave up and his descent from the tree and then the hillside told a story; broad shoulders drooping, arms hanging as if without muscle or bone, back strained beyond redemption and a glazed look in his brown eyes. Then again, it was amazing how rapidly we recovered after a short rest and sustenance. On our first day we harvested three large trees and filled a sack and three-quarters that weighed about a hundred and twenty kilos. Driving home we were quite stunned with exhaustion yet filled with pride at our achievement — our minds so busy coping with our various aches and pains that we could hardly speak.

As always, arrival at Villa Olga was a pleasure. Jupiter and Titbits were there to greet us followed in quick succession by Europa and Tiger-Tim, a terracotta cat with beautiful markings and a recent arrival – Purring Pumpkin a delightfully friendly marmalade cat. What a welcome. Several of them jumped up and sat on the car bonnet trying to reach us before winding themselves around our legs that felt as if they had turned to jelly. Homecoming was always a joyous occasion. Nathalie of course, was always there to join in the cats' welcome.

A hot shower and a change of clothes followed by a well-charged vodka and fresh orange juice and we felt fine, muscles obviously well used but otherwise unprotesting. That would come the next day. And such a sense of satisfaction for there is something about harvesting olives that defies description; perhaps the knowledge that it has been done for aeons though not with our motorised poles to be sure but the result has been the same, gives one a sense of continuity, of history almost. Next day we were certainly stiff and sore. We stayed at the villas but did not exactly rest as Mikalis was in a hurry to get the new villa painted before the tilers arrived; he had been unable to get labourers anywhere so the three of us painted for the entire day. That *was* a strain and by the evening I thought my arms were going to fall off they ached so much and I remember thinking once again,

'Well, Valerie, you wanted a new and different life and you sure have got it. Stop complaining and get on with it!'

*

Harvesting olives is a family event and we were frequently hailed by families from the oldest to the youngest with their cavalcades of mules, their side-saddles piled, high with sacks and beating sticks. They often appeared with several goats with heavy udders tethered to the saddles, the daily milk supply or out for a day of good grazing on the clover? Trucks and the rather quaint three-wheeled motorised carts known as 'put-puts' that Cretan farmers use, passed by laden with nets and sacks; this was a rich olive growing area and everyone was out in force. Often there was a certain incongruity in the families themselves; a little round woman carrying an enormous pile of nets stumped past going uphill and greeted us cheerily; she had bright green eyes.

"Pou eínai o Micháli?" Where is Mikalis? she demanded. We replied that he was *árrostos,* unwell, and pointed to our elbows; he had damaged a muscle or tendon and could not work for a while.

She said, *"Ntropí!"* Ntropi! Shame! And charged off up the hill. Shortly after, a smartly dressed woman in her forties with stylishly cut hair and the same bright green eyes into view. She was not carrying anything and looked so un-Cretan that after the initial greeting I asked her if she was from Crete. She nodded and said,

"Nai," which means 'Yes' in this contrary language — and told us that she was the older woman's daughter and owned a shop in Agios Nikolaos and added, shrugging her elegantly padded shoulders,

"In harvest time we must all to help."
She did look quite out of place. Close on her heels was an emaciated elderly man, handsome in a way but well used and somewhat the worse for wear; I could smell the alcohol on his breath from ten yards away; I grinned at Julian and he nodded with amusement. The old man would not be of much use to his family; perhaps he could sit down in the shade and sort out the twigs. Nothing more demanding than that, I fancied. Mid-afternoon as Julian and I were enjoying our baked potatoes and sweet, firm-skinned tomatoes, the same man staggered down the hill and up the valley road to a parked vehicle. On his return, he stopped by our fire and muttered something quite incoherent as he swayed above us. I was about to offer him a mug of coffee when he pulled out a bottle and a small cup from a filthy shoulder bag and poured Julian a shot of raki, indicating with a mischievous wink of his red-rimmed eye amongst other things, that it was warm to drink — and I thought I caught the words δυνατός, thinatos, strong, and γυναίκες, yinekes, women, but he was

impossible to understand, articulate speech being beyond him at this stage. He stood there smiling benignly as Julian knocked the fiery liquid back in one gulp, gasping as it went down his throat then he insisted on me having some and watched with obvious delight as I sipped it, coughing and spluttering and I can put on a good act when called upon. He appeared to be disappointed when I refused politely to have any more. We thanked him profusely and he bowed in a most gentlemanly way, almost falling forward on his face as he did so before continuing on his slow journey up the hill. I hoped he would find his family and a shady tree.

This morning was our fourth sortie to the olive grove. The weather had once more favoured us with warm sunshine and brilliant azure skies — another day for composing sonnets and lying amidst the sea of yellow clover flowers as the bees buzzed around. I remarked to my son that if we had to pick olives then at least we did it in the most supremely satisfying surroundings — Beethoven Spring Sonata country. Spiritually rewarding. I had included a small bottle of raki with our provisions, recalling the amazingly hot glow and the subsequent lifting of tired spirits and muscles following the old man's gift to us, so when we finally sat on the warm stone wall devouring our baked potatoes doused with salt pepper and butter, we gave ourselves a good swig and agreed that there was nothing better for two exhausted and non-Cretan olive pickers than a small shot of Cretan firewater.

"Long live the grape!" we cried as we toasted one another.

"And the olive harvesters!"

We added, lying back on the grass for a short rest, content under the warm sun realising that we had harvested four trees. Yes, four trees — proving that raki works and that we had slaved almost nonstop for nine hours. There *is* a certain urgency in that the olives are ripening fast with the warmer weather; the rain is holding off and they must be harvested without delay; however, we agreed on the way home that we would not harvest four trees in a day again, certainly not trees with a heavy crop. It was just too taxing. What surprised me was that the *brain* was affected by physical activity and after a certain stage of exhaustion it refused to function properly. We were unable to communicate intelligibly by the end of the day yet after all olive picking is not brainwork, just calls for brawn. Nathalie was worried briefly.

A week later we accompanied Mikalis to the processing plant, a huge barn of a place with freezing draughts and throbbing machinery; sadly there are few original olive oil presses left in Crete, everything is mechanised and noisy. We watched with pride as 'our' olives were rapidly transformed into rich green olive oil. The process that takes about ninety minutes is surprisingly simple and is done through a series of huge metal pipes above eye level; a wind machine blows out the leaves and the olives are crushed into a grey, greasy-looking sludge that is then spun to separate it from the pure oil. This oil which still contains sediment is spun with hot water and separated, spun again and the oil drips down into cylindrical containers that are then weighed. We picked about three hundred kilos of olives which were converted into fifty-six kilos of oil as fluid is measured in kilos in Greece. The processing plant is privately owned, operates only four months of the year and charges a processing fee of eight per cent. What impressed me about the procedure is that nothing is wasted; a bit like the pig where only the squeal is not used. The leaves are sold for fodder; the sludge is drained and dried and fuels the hot water tanks used for the separation process and the bulk is sold to another factory that further squeezes out crude oil for soap and non-culinary purposes. I do however, feel a bit sorry for olive trees. They spend the entire year sustaining their beautiful shiny fruit only to have it cruelly whacked off by humans with beating sticks and rotating poles. Their reward is a harsh thrashing each winter — then every second year or so a Draconian pruning to ensure another good crop so that someone can thrash it off its branches once again. Nonetheless it is some comfort to know that every scrap of the olive is used for the benefit of man and beast.

Mikalis in his generosity has insisted we keep the lot. He was unable to find anyone else to reap the harvest and was happy that *we* reap, in more ways than one, the benefits. This shortage of manpower in the winter is a problem all over Crete; one of the main reasons is that young Cretans refuse to harvest olives. Having worked all summer in the tourist trade they are either too tired and/or too rich by the end of the season to do anything else. In winter they rest, thus acres and acres of olives go to waste each year. Any strong man or woman can be certain of work during December and January anywhere in Crete, and most probably elsewhere in Greece as well, but they need to have staying power. Our slight predicament is that we now own a large quantity of virgin olive oil picked by our own fair hands; we could sell it at five hundred drachmas a kilo and could do with the money, but we have developed a sentimental attachment to this particular oil so have decided to keep it. It is after all the first fruit of our labours.

CHAPTER TWELVE

WINTER MUSINGS
A slippery ride and exit one stonemason

It is February — but maybe I should call this chapter 'spring musings' since the almond trees are out in lacy white blossom, the apricots are covered in fat pink and white buds and along the roadsides yellow-centred chamomile daisies vie with the yellow clover still in bright bloom after two months of continuous flowering. The countryside is a picture and I believe I bore my family to snores by enforcing stops so I can investigate and pick a bunch of newly arrived wildflowers. I love daisies. Their simplicity and honesty appeal to me and every spare jam jar and glass holds a bunch of cheerful white chamomile daisies. I also like sunflowers for the same reason. Last week I was beside myself with delight when I spied the first scarlet poppy amongst soft mauve anemones — and now irises and purple orchids are showing above the lush grass. The gorse with its prickly spikes is in bloom dotting the hillsides with splashes of vibrant saffron.

On the rocky terraces, there are tall pale pink bracts of wildflowers that stand stiff and straight, they resemble Michaelmas daisies but when picked they smell like cat's wee. One evening I put some in a vase in front of the large wooden-framed mirror which reflects the elegant living room in Villa Two and the next morning woke to find Julian sniffing irritably and muttering,

"Those bloody cats — they've sprayed around somewhere and the place stinks!"

It did, but we couldn't find any trace of cat spray; we mopped the floors with disinfectant, left doors and windows wide open and did all the things one does when confronted with that acrid and overpowering smell of cats' urine — but nothing helped. Jupiter and Tiger Tim whom Mikalis calls *Ziger Zim*, being unable to pronounce the letter 't', received short shrift from us all as we were convinced it had to be the male cats doing the spraying. They skulked around outside giving us old-fashioned looks when we passed by but we stayed firm and it wasn't until the pink flowers faded and I threw them out, that we discovered that *they* were the culprits. I tried to identify them but failed.

*

Musings — on the fleeting beauty of the almond. Tim, my composer friend arrived one day from England; dressed in shorts and a cotton shirt he spent the remainder of the day extolling the benefits of the Cretan winter. It was so much warmer here than in England he said. I was finding the low temperatures and cold wind uncomfortably cool and a bit of a shock, being unused to a northern winter. But it was February and to be expected Mikalis told me, brown eyes twinkling.

A few days later on my birthday, we took Tim up to the small and unspoiled hamlet of *Pano Elounda,* Upper Elounda, just a few kilometres up the hill from the port of Elounda. The road winds through hundreds of almond trees in full bloom, their delicate flowers transforming the old village into a fairyland with its simple square Cretan cottages with grey smoke curling out of their makeshift chimneys, ancient weathered stone walls, donkeys anchored to olive trees and sleeping cats. We stopped in silence taking in the scene; it was breathtakingly beautiful and I lamented the fact that Nathalie was working and was not with us. A week later we took her to see the trees but all the flowers were gone, replaced by sharp green leaves, delicate in themselves but not the fairyland we had promised her. So transitory is the beauty of spring that one must catch it when one can.

*

Musings — on the failure of Buttercup on a wet and slippery hill. One evening following a rainy afternoon the sky cleared so we took Tim up to the high saddle in the break in the hills above Elounda to see the windmills and the view. A muddy track led temptingly down around the hillside and as usual, on seeing a new road and the prospect of finding yet another magical hidden place Julian decided to see where it led. We followed the narrow road around the hill through terraced stands of olives still dripping with rain as the hillside fell away and we could see across the Bay of Elounda to Spinalonga Island. The view was spectacular; the square white building-block houses of the port reduced to miniature, gleaming in the evening sun following the curve of the bay. Julian continued to drive, sliding a bit as the road grew steeper along the edge of the hill with Tim breathing nervously,

"Christ — do you think we should go on?" while I waxed lyrical on the landscape lying far beneath us. The reply from our driver was,

"Well there's no choice, we can't turn here anyway!"

And we couldn't. On one side of the narrow track was a stone wall holding up a terrace of olives and on the other, the land fell away dramatically and somewhat threateningly. What if we should skid I asked myself briefly but faith in my son's driving stood firm as we went on, wondering where the road would take us. Well! It didn't take us anywhere. We reached a level patch where it widened and stopped abruptly, the muddy ground thick with damp clover and thyme — or was it sage? Its pungency filled the clear air as we wandered around.

"Suppose this is where they turned their vehicles around during harvesting," someone said.

"Or their donkeys," someone else said.

Looking back up the hill we realised there would be problems, Buttercup's tyres were very narrow and not made for gripping steep and slippery surfaces; they simply spun in the thick mud and Buttercup didn't budge, so I drove — rather hung on to the wheel like grim death as it literally twisted around in my hands as Julian and Tim began to push. Tim lasted only a few moments, not being quite as fit or as slim as he might be and that's an understatement. He retired to the roadside panting and sweating and sat on a rock while Julian continued to push, shouting hoarsely, "Keep on, Ma, keep *on!*"

Buttercup's engine screamed in pain as she skidded from side to side almost hitting the stone wall on one side and veering dangerously close to the steep drop on the other, occasionally gaining a few precious yards up the hill. The return journey seemed endless and there were times when I was convinced we were going over the edge as the wheels refused to respond to my steering and we lurched as if driverless, this way and that. How Julian kept his grip on the back of the car was beyond me. The only thing in our favour was that she was a light vehicle with virtually no weight apart from the engine, so was not as heavy to push as she might have been.

It was the most hair-raising experience I have ever had in a car, and I have had some on African and Australian bush roads. My instinct was to abandon the car and start the long trek back to the little hamlet on the other side of the hill, but the light was fading, it was getting cold and misty. Julian kept shoving and shouting and I kept hanging onto the wheel, accelerating and wondering how any engine could withstand such a beating. Finally, the steepest part was over and I hurtled ahead leaving Julian behind, not daring to stop until the ground was level. I ran back to find the two men sitting on some rocks panting and puffing; Julian looked as if he was about to explode and Tim appeared to be somewhat sheepish as he apologised for being so useless. I must say they were both so complimentary about my driving I went around with quite a swollen head for a while.

*

Musings — on birds and whether or not it is spring. It does seem like spring. The sun has changed its light and warmth as an erudite taverna owner described it to us the other day. It has *more* light — a whiter light. We have been gardening and painting the villas wearing shorts and t-shirts, though generally at about midday, just before Nathalie comes back from work a breeze springs up and we wonder why we are lunching on the balcony when it is so cold. The air temperature is still quite low and in an instant, the wind whisks away the morning's warmth and before we can change our clothes we are covered with goose pimples. Yet on other days — with increasing frequency — it remains clear and calm. Longer days now, sunrise at six-thirty and sunset just before six-thirty.

And the birds! Oh the birds, there are so many in the trees at Villa Olga, their song awakens me each morning and accompanies the day. The robin has made its home with us this winter and I am absolutely beside myself with delight; it lives in the olive tree on the terrace below Villa One where I have spent part of the winter and has the skinniest legs and the fattest russet chest and I wonder why do they call him 'robin *red-breast*' when his breast is russet? I suppose 'robin *russet breast*' isn't quite so easy to say? His song is not a song but a series of sharp clicks, more like an interjection which he aims at me through the window as I sit typing. I become aware of his beady eyes looking straight at me from the bare branches of the pomegranate. Perhaps the clicking of the typewriter attracts him or perhaps he thinks I am another large and chatty bird? He must know about the marauding cats as I warn him whenever he appears, and I do not feed him though would dearly love to do so.

I watch a seagull rising on air currents at eye level from the villa above mine where Julian and Nathalie are spending the winter. Living high above the road does have its advantages as we too have a bird's eye view over the plunging hillside below us to the bay. The gull soars gracefully in curves and swirls as if drawing in the sky, always returning to the same spot — perhaps looking down at a mouse amongst the spiny shrubs and bushes. Occasionally it uses its wings lazily and without effort then swerves upwards into yet another air current. My mind races back in time to Greek mythology;

*

Icarus, I understand what you made but you should have used the same design as did Daedalus, your father. Perhaps you did, but you were a highflier weren't you — and closer to the sun you flew. Are you now that graceful sea bird I am seeing with feathered wings?

*

Musings — on a Cretan stonemason. Mikalis has persuaded the old grey-haired stonemason who originally carved the archway and fireplace in the first villa twelve years ago, to return to work on the last villa at the top of the hill. He has the calm and eyes of an artist. Fine-drawn. Sensitive. I suspect he did not want to return to work for Mikalis as he interferes with and dictates vociferously to all the craftsmen and workmen who come to the villas. Invariably they end up quarrelling loudly and often leave in disgust in the middle of a job. At the moment Mikalis is more irritable than usual because his arm is in a sling and I suspect he is in pain. The damage to his elbow requires a month's rest and physiotherapy so he stomps around the terraces, brows drawn together and manages to protest or complain about everything in his path. I do empathise for I am never out of pain. Julian and I avoid him, having tried sympathy which we sincerely feel, but even his great fondness for Julian does not prevent him from being loudly impolite.

The stonemason sits on the floor in the vast unfinished sitting-room and chips away at the grey stone making tiny marks which stand out in paler veins — rather like fossilised moss in stone — then beneath a huge metal frame he builds the grand archway with loving care and attention, all the time being distracted by the argumentative and irascible Mikalis. They squabble ceaselessly — the stonemason ever polite, long-suffering — but I can see he is becoming weary of the interference and I have heard voices raised with increasing frequency. I went up to the villa during one of the cold and windy spells and offered him a hot drink as he sat with the freezing gale whipping around his thin body — there are no doors or windows yet in the villa — but he refused politely and continued chipping with what must have been frozen hands. A hardy stonemason. The Greeks call the wind *anemos* and I mistakenly thought the word animosity came from this source, but it doesn't — animosity is from the Latin, *animus*.

That word animosity was certainly what our stonemason had been feeling towards Mikalis one morning as I could no longer hear his hammer and later Mikalis told me with a face black with rage, that he was gone. No! He raged — he was not coming back and it did not matter that we would not have a fireplace until next winter because spring was on its way. But the fireplace is incomplete and how do we advertise Villa Seven next season? Must think about that tomorrow as Scarlett O'Hara did in *Gone with the Wind*; it is too hard to cope with today.

*

CHAPTER THIRTEEN

CRETAN COOKING
Snails and Greek television

Musings — on the colour blue. I sit in the sun and watch extraordinary cloud patterns being drawn by high winds in different directions; the winds transform and shred the clouds into fine shards this way and that across the deep blue sky. Spectacular and most unusual. I wonder if the colour of the sky is cerulean blue and does it matter? Later I find there are a dozen different shades of blue listed and it could be any of those except for an azure sky since that implies an 'unclouded sky'. I learn something new every day.

Musings — on eating snails. Last year, before Francesca returned to Australia with the solemn promise that she would return in May, Mikalis and Marika took her and Julian to Skinnias, the little village on the north coast of the bay where Marika's parents live. Her father Papa Yiannis is a priest, an amicable and refined gentleman with a long white beard and a fading memory. The couple lives in a cottage with an outside kitchen where the only sign of the presence of an undoubtedly rich son-in-law is an outsize fridge in one of the bedrooms and a large television set. The village, perhaps hamlet would be a more appropriate term, like many on the island is dying. Once a busy settlement there are now only eighty inhabitants, all elderly and I wonder what will happen to these gradually disappearing sad remnants of rural Crete. We have explored many of them, wandered around crumbling stone walls and collapsing wooden beams, old ovens full of wildflowers with ceramic chimney pots lying amongst the herbs. Not even a feral cat to be seen but I can feel the memories somehow and they make me sad. Wistful.

On their return, Francesca launched into a bright and detailed description of their outing and I felt as if I had been with them. Mikalis drove towards a little beach and stopped in an olive grove and began to collect snails — the ground was covered with them and when he suggested that they did likewise, they asked where they should put them. He indicated their pockets would suffice. Francesca has always had a somewhat queasy stomach and she told me on her return, that it was then that she started feeling a bit nauseous, expecting that there was worse to come. There was! On satisfying himself that they had collected sufficient snails Mikalis took them back to the cottage and Marika's mother boiled them in salty water before offering them round as a delicacy.

"Did you eat them?" I asked incredulously.

"Yes," they responded.

"We really had to; it would have been rude to refuse. Just as well Cretans don't use snail-bait!" Julian observed wryly.

Apparently they tasted like rubber tyres cooked in salt and oil, not too revolting fortunately for Francesca, who might well have regurgitated the entire contents of her stomach as she has been known to do on many occasions. I recall with amusement a rule we tried to implement in our Canberra house when the children were growing up. We have always had cats, mainly Burmese or Tonkinese — a cross-breed of Siamese and Burmese — and Clothilde, one of our many cats had a habit of being sick during the night; this usually occurred on the mat in the passageway between the bedrooms and just in front of the bathroom that everyone visited first thing in the morning. The understanding was that whoever saw the nauseating pile first, should clean it up. In retrospect it was of course the silliest rule I could have dreamed up as obviously no one admitted to *ever* noticing the pile of sick! However, I always knew if Francesca had seen it *she* would have ended up with her head in the basin, throwing up. She was also quite hopeless when Amanda and Philippa her two sisters, aged eight and ten years younger than she, needed a nappy change or would regurgitate their morning Farex; almost anything would turn her stomach, poor girl. She is still somewhat sensitive she tells me though one day having a family of her own will toughen her up no doubt.

Back to Mikalis and snails! They returned late that night having phoned to say they would be delayed and when they arrived, they reeked of raki and were in high spirits, literally and metaphorically speaking. They had stopped off at a modern house belonging to one of Mikalis' friends and naturally enough, had been invited in for a drink. The interior was almost bare but for a table and rickety chairs in the sparse kitchen and in the passage, they noticed a live chicken standing in a plastic bag tied up to its neck and tethered to the door handle — a curious method of preventing a chicken from straying or was it simply waiting to be the next meal poor thing?

*

Musings — on confused Cretan cockerels who do not know whether it's day or night. The two-storey Cretan household next door has a veritable menagerie of caged birds of every description, many of them songbirds but also, in a rambling broken-down run on the Villa Olga side of his house, chickens, ducks, guinea-fowl, turkeys and rabbits, all shaded by a spreading carob tree. The stench when the wind comes from that direction is something chronic and I have complained to Mikalis who just smiles and says they are friends; I have asked the owner Giorgios if he can do something about it, but he affects not to understand. The caged birds on their balcony and in the aviary make a pretty sound and seem content enough, though my instinct when I see a bird in a cage is to open the door and let it fly away. I have strong memories of growing up in tropical coastal Dar es Salaam when the natives — unwisely — came round to our house to sell their bright parakeets I would chatter away and distract them while accidentally on purpose open the cage door and let the birds loose, then recompense them for their loss. The urge remains strong. No wild creature should be deprived of its freedom.

Also next door there is a cockerel that crows with a strangled and harsh sound day and night; it squawks not only at full moon — when everything crows, barks, howls or miaows and humans including myself are restless and filled with curious energy — but also at odd hours in the middle of the night long before dawn and — unforgivably — during siesta, two to five pm when any self-respecting Cretan bird should know that silence is required, nay *demanded.* It would be difficult to bear if it were an ordinary cockerel crow, but this one comes out half-strangled as if some desperate person has had a go at him and indeed, tried to strangle the wretched thing and failed. One of these days or nights I may well complete the job.

Musings — on Cretan dogs that are tethered and probably suffer from amongst other things, intense boredom. There is some kudos in owning a dog Yiannis tells me. Giorgios has three; two are attractive beagles and the third is a hunting dog. All are tethered. All bored and barking. Giorgios is a kindly, gentle-looking man who sings when he has had an evening out; he has white crinkly hair, pale eyes behind glasses and works above the bus station. When he goes out with his dogs a metamorphosis takes place; he wears a camouflage safari jacket and trousers, big boots and even his body language changes as he controls his hysterically excitable hounds on their leashes. Some deep-seated instinct takes over as he strides over the brow of the hill accompanied by the shrill barks and yelps of his hunting hounds — perhaps they stem from his hunter-gatherer days not so long ago on this island. Even now he becomes the hunter with a killer instinct after a hare or feathered creature on which to feed his family

The villagers of Ellinika have many dogs. In the main they are thin of spine, tan of colour and anxious to be friendly to any passer-by and bark and bark I am positive from sheer boredom. Early morning is the worst time; they set up a cacophonous chorus that no Cretan appears to hear. It is background music to their ears but to us, it is a constant invasion of our craving for peace and quiet now and then; they also invade the sanctity of siesta. I have been up to the village on hot afternoons amidst the accompanying shriek of the cicadas nearly driven mad by the incessant yapping and barking, but it's like visiting the dead as no one is awake but the bored dogs and me. Mostly they are hunting dogs and when the season begins, they accompany their gun-bearing masters in their smart hunters' gear over the hillsides and mercifully disappear for hours.

What heaven that must be for them — allowed to run and chase at last after months of inactivity for no one would dream of taking their dogs for a daily walk, or even let them loose so they can run around occasionally. And most of all, their families need to augment their diets with protein which doesn't grow in the ground. I always wish them well in their hunt, yet the very idea of hunting is an anathema to me as it is to the rest of the family. Some dogs do not enjoy the freedom of the hunt, they are mere guard dogs; one female in particular in Ellinka at the top of our hill has captured my attention and overwhelming sympathy and sadness at the appalling conditions under which she is kept. She is a charming creature, pale tan with appealing brown eyes that speak to me whenever she sees me approach; painfully thin with ribs sticking out she spends her days on a round up-turned wooden drum and sleeps in a giant earthenware pot that lies on its side. The rope that ties her is cruelly short. She belongs to a pair of incredibly ancient and bent sisters who live in two single rooms next door to each other in a tumble-down cottage and when we pass by on our evening walks accompanied by all the cats, this beguiling creature wags her tail frantically and whines and smiles, almost turning inside-out with delight at our presence. My heart goes out to her and occasionally I give her a bone to gnaw, wishing as I do that, I could undo her rope and take her with me to the villa for some badly needed loving care and sufficient food to cover her staring skeleton — and get rid of the worms that certainly infest her. I have had to harden my heart and not pay her too frequent attention for I fear it may interfere with the familiar and Spartan pattern of her life. She is one of the many barkers and I am sure she is trying to tell the world that she is bored and wants to fly over the hills and valleys chasing the wild hare. Little brown-eyed Cretan dog, you lost out this time around — maybe next time life will be better?

I can't seem to get over my distress by the conditions under which this dear little dog lives — or is the more appropriate word "survives?" I tell myself I must try to understand the harsh conditions the Cretans have suffered through the years, particularly the elderly many of whom are the inhabitants of this little hamlet behind these villas; their dog is there to guard them, to bark if someone approaches and the old girls come to the door, anxious-eyed to see what is going on and perhaps fearing for their safety? It is heart-breaking but they are not deliberately cruel, it has always been thus. I must remind myself of this factor, but it is difficult.

Musings — on Cretan cooking. We have had some interesting concoctions this winter. Mikalis has planted rows of winter cabbages that do not form hearts, one eats the leaves and the yellow florets;

endive which must be cooked with several changes of water to remove the bitterness; a wild cos lettuce that is only edible after similar treatment and lots of spinach. Wild onions have sprung up all over the garden; they look like leeks but their flavour is too strong for our palates. Mikalis has shown us how to choose the good dandelions and their flowers — they need to be picked before they are old, and these boiled up for about an hour then served with liberal quantities of olive oil, lemon juice and salt make an earthy and tasty vegetable. He calls them all *horta* — a generic term for these wild vegetables which were once weeds to us and that includes all kinds of indigenous plants growing over the hillsides. One often comes across *yia-yias,* little old ladies with baskets full of *horta* and large bunches of other vegetables that are sold at the Wednesday markets. We have learned not to throw away beetroot tops but to simmer them for about ten minutes in the same water as the beets and serve with oil and lemon juice; quite delicious and their rich colour adds a certain aesthetic value to the rest of the food on the plate. No wonder the Cretans are renowned for reaching a great age. Their diet for centuries was vegetables, fruit, fish, goat and sheep's milk and cheese and rarely, red meat — mutton or goat — the former indulged upon mainly at Easter. Sadly today's Cretans are not as healthy Mikalis' wife Marika tells us their diets have become westernised with an over-abundance of red meat, sugar in its various forms, dairy products plus fast foods, and that the young were healthier before these additions to the daily fare. She blames the American influence for everything.

Dried salted cod that lies smothered in rough rock salt in wooden casks in the little stores makes a tasty and ridiculously cheap dish when cooked with herbs in a slow oven with leeks, potatoes, carrots and parsley. However it needs to be soaked overnight initially to remove the salt, and I didn't realise this so produced a meal which was inedible; even the cats turned their noses up at it.

One afternoon Mikalis announced his intention to bring *hirinés brizóles,* pork chops, for supper and he would cook them on the open fire. We were to do nothing! He and Marika arrived loaded with supplies including litres of village wine in a filthy plastic sump oil container and the chops that had been marinaded in wine and garlic for two whole days Marika explained, as we raved about the flavour after Mikalis had cooked them over the hot coals. Julian had taken it upon himself to prepare Cretan style chips that are cut through the centre into flat ovals together with a large Greek salad and crusty chunks of bread. We had a superb evening and managed to converse surprisingly well given our limited Greek vocabulary. After they left, we lounged in front of the fire agreeing that it had made a pleasant change in mid-winter when we saw few people, especially at night. I believe Mikalis would like to return to live at Villa Olga again but Marika won't hear of it. She prefers the town where she spends a lot of her time on their little balcony keeping a check on the daily activities of its inhabitants; she is a sharp-eyed and I suspect, sharp-tongued woman and I have gathered is one of the town gossips.

Musings — on Greek television. There are only two channels in eastern Crete yet in Heraklion in central Crete, there are five. Something to do with the mountain range I gather. The channel with the best films and occasional documentary fades out more often than it is visible and when we complain to all and sundry they say,

Oh yes we know, Channel Two has always been like that," and when we ask if anyone has ever complained about this they reply,

"Yes — of course! But nothing can be done about it!"

Our amazement is compounded when we discover that the problem has been present for *five* years. The final comment is that no one *ever* watches Channel Two. They say,

"If there is nothing to watch on Channel One, we hire a video for the evening."

Another disappointing factor is the late start of all films. The earliest time is at ten-thirty and every film is interrupted by the news at midnight which runs for half an hour — plus advertisements — so one loses the thread of any plot. Consequently we seldom see the second half of any film; we look at one another in despair and retire to bed rather than suffer the thirty-minute interruption.

Musings — on boundaries. I find it intriguing that the two shady carob trees above the new villa on our property do not belong to Mikalis but to Giorgios, his neighbour. It is quite common to own a tract of land yet not necessarily the trees growing on that land. The rows of almonds so pretty in white lacy flower are not ours but belong to Giorgios although they are on our property.

Musings — on the generation gap. Giorgios' mother is one of the many bent old women of the tiny hamlet of Ellinika that sits just over the hill; she and the others wander around our terraces at dawn collecting *horta* and baskets of clover; she also owns the goat Dame Edith Sitwell and milks her each evening. Her son and our only neighbour, appears to have leapt ahead of his simple village upbringing by several centuries with his middle-class house and lifestyle; yet the same generosity and concern for his fellowman remain strong for he frequently gives us fresh eggs, half a loaf of special sweet bread made for some feast or other. In return, we push his little car when the battery is flat, which is often and we enjoy a good neighbourly relationship that we all value. I did wonder though, last summer what his old mother thought of the topless girls lying around our pool. She spent many an afternoon leaning over their balcony that overlooks the pool watching the young and old cavorting and carrying on — often joining in with their laughter, putting her dark brown hand over her mouth and turning away as she laughs.

I wish I could speak to her properly but my Greek remains superficial and I am frustrated as I cannot find a teacher; I do study on my own and sometimes with Julian and Nathalie, but I feel in need of a tutor. I had an excellent one last year for two months but he left to go to Canada. Come back Dimitris, I need you! He had a love and aesthetic understanding of the purity of his language and imparted it so well and with such enthusiasm and the origins of the title 'A Cricket in the Wind' came from him; he likened my frenetic activities while running the villas to being like a cricket in the wind. We all resemble crickets in the wind as we dart around doing this and that throughout the day and the long night hours. And we love it.

Musings — on winter gardening. The battle of the clover continues. All the terraces are now weeded, dug up with soil overturned mostly by hard-working Nathalie and planted with various cuttings and joy oh joy, hundreds of seedlings are coming up; marigolds will be in plague proportions; zinnias; bachelor's buttons; sunflowers; stock — a favourite with the Greeks; and self-seeded tobacco plants that last summer filled the terraces with their heavy perfume and multi-coloured flowers. The citrus trees are in full bud, their scent already quite heady and overpowering and the apricots resemble brides with their pink and white flowers; the pale yellow unscented jasmine sends long sprays across the path and the bright berries of the spectacular shrub Pyracantha, also known as Firethorn for obvious reasons, contain small amounts of a cyanide-like compound but are not considered poisonous. It attracts some bird species that regularly eat the decorative berries.

The winter garden is full of colour though not quite as vibrant as in summer — more subdued, politer somehow — and the geraniums and bougainvillaea have not ceased to bloom. When we arrived I noticed there was little variety in the flowers Mikalis had planted — he concentrated on fruit trees, flowering shrubs and creepers — and I've noted with satisfaction that he is impressed with the rapidity with which we have transformed the baking red earth terraces beneath the trees into bright borders of flowering plants. He occasionally arrives with a few small stock seedlings that he admits he has pilfered from someone's garden as he does a backward, downward curving movement with his hand and says, κλέφτης, kleftis, thief!

Last year's night-scented stocks are heavy with their clotted cream flowers of white, purple and magenta and I note outside Villa Four that hibiscus buds are forming. There are also new bracts of flowers on the purple bougainvillaea in the vast pot by the steps up to the swimming pool terrace. The hyacinth bulbs I planted in November have been flowering for several weeks now; their cloying fragrance pervades the air and I have observed Mikalis lean down and take a deep sniff on occasions. He has a passion as do I, for heavily scented blooms and he waxes quite lyrical over the long-stemmed purple and deep mustard-coloured freesias that lean over onto the path. A few tiny grape hyacinths have decided they alone do not like the soil I have planted them in — otherwise, success reigns in our winter garden. It appears there is no dormant season in Crete.

Before I move on I have to mention the ranunculi corms I introduced just before Christmas; the plants stand beneath several lemon trees laden with next season's buds and already ripening lemons and several ranunculi have opened into striking many-petalled yellow flowers with ruby-red centres; they are quite beautiful and catch the eye with their elegant splendour. I planted five corms close together and asked them to flower at the same time to make a real show, but two of the five have fat secretive buds that I desperately want to prise open with my fingers to see what colour they are. I want a show, not an apology from them! Patience Valerie, patience. Maybe next year they will all flower at once.

I am trying to learn all the names of the European shrubs and trees but there are so many that are unfamiliar to me, having never lived in the northern hemisphere before. One Greek word for which I have a fondness and remember with ease is the Greek word for 'rose', *triandáfilo,* thirty leaves; trianda means thirty and the word *filo* as in filo pastry means 'leaves'.

I put some grapevine cuttings into a vase recently and now thread-like roots are showing and green frilly-edged leaves are starting to curl from the knobbly stems — such a surge of energy and new life all around me. How wonderful nature is and how blessed I am to be able to appreciate and savour it without being rushed off my feet.

Musings — on winter weather. I asked a Cretan friend if the warm spell we were having meant an end to winter. He lifted his head and chin upwards in the Greek negative way, rolled his eyes and said *Ochi!* No! before quoting an old Greek adage about March being bad for wood — meaning more wood is needed in March, and suddenly today we have again been plunged into wintry conditions. Last night we were struck by the wildest winds, gusting and keening through the telephone wires or whatever those overhead wires are that festoon the road edges. I was reminded of the sighing and moaning of the winds in *Wuthering Heights* with a suspicion of handsome Heathcliffe lurking around in the dark and shifting shadows. I love any kind of real weather — the wilder the better. I like to be reminded that the elements are alive and well and I enjoy walking up the slope behind the villas with the wind on my face, better still if it is raining and I can feel the cold stinging rain on my cheeks; I find it incredibly invigorating and want to walk forever — far into the mountains. On these windy days when the *meltemi* — that dry wind that blows from north to northwest across the Aegean Sea — blows hard and no ferries or planes come to the island and Crete is often cut off for days on end. This morning it is seriously bitterly cold and far below the bay is chopped up into shades of grey and black with white-topped waves that we know as 'white horses' but which the Greeks call charmingly 'lamb's tails.' The birds are still and silent, hiding in a protected place. I would sum up the Cretan winter weather as being capricious — there is no other word to describe the extreme ends of the spectrum we experience. Fortunately the cold spells only last three to four days at the most — if it were any longer the Cretans would throw themselves into the bay in despair. Followed by me!

Musings — on the rain. The locals are worried about the lack of rain this season. They say it has been abnormally hot and dry during January and February; water shortages are forecast for the coming summer and already the water mains are turned off for hours each day, and I hear the reservoir outside Athens on the mainland is running dry. The snow on the Dikte Mountains is melting during the warm spells and while this fills the reservoirs, more rain is needed for the fruit and vegetable crops and of course — the olives. I hope our beautiful garden will not suffer this summer; so much loving care has gone into it not to mention hard physical labour from Julian and Nathalie who have worked tirelessly digging over the hard-baked earth of the many terraces. Later— after planting some spectacular flowering plants no doubt, standing with hands on aching backs and smiling at the fruits of their labour.

Musings — on wild cypresses. One morning Julian and I explored the sloping rocky hillside that plunges into the bay below our villas and continued to investigate an interesting looking plateau at the edge of the cliffs. It was a well-grazed area with a collapsing grey stone wall beside an empty stone well with steps leading down to darkness; far below beyond the enclosing arms of the wall the hill sloped steeply to the cliff edge across small level terraces each surrounded by low stone walls, obviously the remains of an old settlement. Several large carobs stood in a semi-circle and in the nearby ravine we were thrilled to discover wild cypresses in between the terraced olives. They grew thickly in the depth of the ravine down to the sea. There are so few left on Crete, a ship-building empire from Minoan times and the island has been gradually depleted of its massive cypress forests. Fires and the introduction of the goat have prevented seedlings from generating that has left the island virtually without natural forest, yet they once covered Crete even to the tops of the tallest mountains.

William Lithgow writes in his book 'The Rare Adventures and Painful Peregrinations of William Lithgow' (1632)

"Mount Ida is the highest mountain in Crete and by the computation of shepherds' feet amounteth to six miles in height. It is over-clad, even to the top, with cyprus trees."

Sadly no longer. The wild cypress is reduced to the steep gorges and gullies and the mountains are mainly barren. I understand the only full-sized cypresses grow in the Samaria Gorge in western Crete beside a small church named Agios Nikolaos, the patron saint of seafarers, but I have yet to see them. We were so delighted to discover the green plateau, the olive terraces and cypresses so close to home that Julian and I erected a small stone cairn and vowed we would one day buy this piece of land that juts out into the bay with its unimpeded view of the Thripte Mountains. We would build two villas, one for me and one for him and Nathalie. He planned to bring her to see the site when she returned from town that evening, but I do not know if he ever did. In my mind it already belonged to us. When I think of leaving Crete the thought floats away like almond blossom on the wind; it does not seem possible that I shall live anywhere else, but what the gods have in store for me I do not know. *Carpe diem*, a phrase that comes from the Roman poet Horace, means literally 'Pluck the day' though is usually translated as 'Seize the day'. This I know and attempt to adhere to.

"It will all come out in the wash," my mother used to say — but I never found out exactly *what* it was that would come out. I am still waiting, but she has gone to join my father and that belief fills me not with sadness but with a calm quiet joy that they are together once more; for how else can one deal with the departure of two greatly adored parents?

CHAPTER FOURTEEN

THE VANISHING POLICE STATION
Further battles and red tape

I have deliberately avoided mentioning the difficult times we experienced during our initial months in Crete; we were hounded by delays and frustrations, incorrect and conflicting advice followed by gloom and despondency that was dispelled only by the glory of each day that somehow put everything into perspective. Who cares if the last appointment with Sophia, our charming lawyer was interrupted six times by people in cars who stopped by her window to consult her on some problem or other, or passers-by popping into her office and standing between us as though we were invisible; others to pay bills; the telephone constantly ringing — she had an answerphone, why didn't she use it I kept asking myself — not to mention two short consultations with Greeks who were in a hurry and did we mind? Then one of her immediate relatives was taken to Heraklion hospital and the office was closed for ten days. Do these delays *really* matter?

And as for Manolis! Yes another Manolis. Julian remarked wryly that if someone stood in the small square in Agios Nikolaos and shouted "Manoli" — the final 's' is always dropped off in the vocative — every second car would stop and most of the shopkeepers would come out of their shops in response. It is the commonest name in this region followed closely by Yiannis. The name of the grandfather is wished on the grandson so there is little variety in male Christian names in Greece. As I was saying *this* Manolis was a bull-necked man with sloping shoulders and a chronic liver complaint who dominated the Aliens Police Department and who had an obvious distaste for non-Cretans. I do not blame him, in fact he has my sympathy because his island is being swamped with foreigners, so many of them undesirable 'yobbos' of varying nationalities and is in danger of losing its identity. If I were in a position of power I would behave exactly as Manolis does. However, I am not and I am at his mercy and he has used this to our disadvantage until he has almost driven me — all of us — to despair.

The saga is never-ending; the journeys up the concrete stairs to the office either to find that Manolis is not there — he has many acres of vines in the Siteia regions that he tends to visit frequently we are told, or he is fixing his car — or if he happens to be present, he will look at whatever piece of paper I have brought him, grunt then mutter in Greek that I should return tomorrow or next week or get another piece of paper. When I ask him where I can find this piece of paper that will allow him to get on with giving us our permit, he will shrug his shoulders and then affect to read something in front of him and I am summarily and rudely dismissed. I remarked to a friend who has been in Crete for five years that trying to establish oneself in Greece is a real test of strength and determination. She agreed and did nothing to cheer me up by saying it really *was* never-ending; something or other tended to crop up just as one thought the way was clear and once again one would be at the mercy of these bureaucrats who were doing their level best to send us back from whence we came, or for whom *avrio,* tomorrow, was their credo.

I think one of the main stumbling blocks apart from the fact that months go past and nothing is finalised, is the stubborn refusal of any public servant to take responsibility for anything if it can be avoided. They categorically refuse to put anything down in writing in case at some future date, someone might hold them responsible for their decision. They will agree verbally but if you ask them for it in writing — up goes the head and eyebrows, the mouth turns down, chin juts out and the negative *óchi* is mouthed.

Finally, with Yiannis' assistance I acquire a tax number, a set of books and register Villa Olga as a business. Unbelievably the contract is finally signed, sealed and settled; much shaking of hands and broad smiles and a commemorative photograph taken with Mikalis and Marika and it seems as if we are finally legitimate. I find an English-speaking accountant and together with my medical book cleanly stamped I front up to Manolis, practising my Greek in the car and feeling quite determined not to let his surly manner intimidate me as it had in the past. He had given me a list of requirements; I had fulfilled them to the letter or so I thought. He is surly as I arrive. Looks up, recognises me then quickly turns away. I approach with a forced smile on my face and a cheery, *"Kalimera, Kirie Manoli,"* on my lips.

He mutters something, glances at the papers I have placed in front of him then pushes them away irritably. Where was my permission from the Tourist Police to run my villas? I say they have permitted me to run the business through Yiannis. Where was my office he demands? At Villa Olga, I reply. That was not good enough. I *had* to have an office in town. I am astonished. This has never been mentioned before and I gape at him speechlessly then leave angrily, wishing I had more Greek, wishing I had never come to Crete and beginning to despair at ever winning the battle.

That evening over copious glasses of red with the family my gloom gradually fades as the sun sets and once again I realise that no matter how hard it is proving to be, we have definitely come to stay and no jumped-up, hungover policeman was going to stop us. I return the next day and point out that I am taking over a villa business that has been running for five years without an office in town so why then did I need one? I have my office, a phone, a secretary — myself — a typewriter, and as all our visitors are overseas bookings which was not quite true, there is no point in having an office seven kilometres away from the villas. He shakes his bullhead irritably and turns away once again. He will need a letter from the Tourist Police he says, permitting me to operate from Villa Olga.

Once again back to Yiannis who runs his fingers through his curly hair and laughs and says that the Tourist Police have already agreed to let me operate from there and that I did not need an office in town.

"But," he cautions. "They will not write a letter to say this."

When I quiz him he chuckles again and says,

"They do not write letters because maybe one day they can get into trouble. And it is too much work anyway!"

I persuade him to accompany me to the Tourist Police who are a pleasant and affable lot residing on the floor above Manolis' — they listen, look serious and exchange comments in rapid Greek that leave me way behind. As we depart, one of the men comes out and speaks to Yiannis; the outcome is unchanged; they agree I do not need premises in town but they will not put this in writing. Stalemate, I think, as I come home. What do I do now? I soothe myself with a cup of *Dictamo* mountain tea and consider the situation. How best to obtain something in writing? By writing to the source and requesting a reply, I think. I phone Yiannis who thinks this is a good idea, so I write a simple letter in English asking permission to have my office at Villa Olga.

My helpful lady lawyer types it up for me in translation at no charge and I take a copy, place the original in an envelope addressed to the Tourist Police on the fourth floor of the building, and the copy to Manolis on the third floor at the Aliens' Police. With Julian for moral support of which I am by now badly in need, I hand the envelopes to the two recipients: Manolis is as bad-tempered as ever and obviously puzzled as he opens the envelope and when he sees the address at the top of the letter which is to the Tourist Police — he is looking at the carbon copy — gives it back to me saying it is *not* for him. I show him his name at the bottom of the letter and try to explain that the *same* letter had gone to two recipients of the Police Department and that his letter was a copy. This is unheard of and he is quite obviously out of his depth.

At that moment the helpful man from the Tourist Police arrives from the floor above holding his letter out to Manolis. He has seen Manolis' name at the bottom of the letter — i.e. *cc Manolis* — and thought the letter was for *him*. They speak for a moment then Manolis hands me back both letters, nods his head almost agreeably and says, "*Ναι ναι καταλαβαίνω*," Ne ne katalaveno, Yes yes I understand, and tells us to come back the next day.

Tomorrow comes and I go to see him but he is away. In hospital they tell me for two days. Come back in two days. I return on the fourth day faint-hearted, feeling quite certain that some other excuse will have been dreamed up in the interim and I wonder once again if I feel strong enough to cope with this man. But he almost smiles at me and sends me to see 'another man on another day' and to bring Yiannis with me.

This I do and we meet the 'other man' who, it transpires actually is the chief whom I'd seen on rare occasions in an office adjacent to Manolis's. It is then that I discover that Manolis is a mere underling. His chief is pleasant and polite and speaks slowly in Greek so that I can understand and tells me that he approves my application and will send it to Athens. He cannot guarantee its approval but thinks there will be no problem. I am to return to see Manolis who will finalise the application. My heart sinks — no — not him again!

Several days later I call in but he is out fixing his car. He will be back the next day. I am there bright and early and for some inexplicable reason Manolis relents just a little as he signs the papers, reams of them, and I discover that he speaks a bit of English. I congratulate him and to my astonishment, he almost blushes. At last I think — a chink in his armour — maybe he does belong to the human race. I thank him heartily as only an English woman can and as I shake his hand I feel a bit like Brown Owl. Before I leave I ask him when I can expect the papers back from Athens. His head and eyebrows tilt back, chin and eyes upwards in a total disclaimer of any knowledge in this direction. I smile and leave, triumphant at last.

Some six weeks later a phone call from Yiannis to tell me the papers have come through and I am finally legitimate. Now I can apply for my five-year residency provided I am able to summon up the strength.

*

When I first applied for my five-year residency it was in November and Manolis and I had reached an understanding. He had come to the conclusion that I was here to stay willy-nilly and that all his negativity and rudeness had achieved little but delays in the inevitable finalising of my papers. He was quite affable on this occasion when I asked, once again, how long it would take for me to become legal; he muttered something about Χριστούγεννα–
Christoyenya, Christmas, and that I should come and see him at the end of January. Two months away. I gulped as the implications sank into my brain because I needed to obtain my residency before I could send for our belongings currently stored in Sydney; these included all our winter clothing, blankets, heaters etcetera which we would now be compelled to purchase. Mikalis provided nothing but bed linen and light Cretan bedspreads as the villas were only equipped for the long hot summers, though he had a few blankets and a fireplace in two of the villas. Like it or not we would have to buy some blankets

and rugs and warm clothes, so we had an enforced shopping spree at the Wednesday market.

Fighting and elbowing one's way through the crowds of early shoppers both men and women had already become a way of life; a kind of frenzy takes place as if the stalls are going to run out of supplies which they never do and the Cretans — mostly the women — practise a form of rib-digging and force their way in front just as you have finally got the attention of the gypsy stallholder and your position is usurped, never to be regained. They prefer to serve their kin before the foreigner although I know the price fluctuates and they make more money out of the non-Cretans. That is until they become acquainted with one, then they greet you with warmth in their brown eyes and you feel you have made yet another friend. It has taken us a while to appreciate though perhaps that is not the right word, that this pushing and shoving and elbowing is the way things are done here. It is definitely *not* first come first served — it is those with the sharpest elbows that are first served while you stand back with your well-bred Anglo-Saxon reserve and wonder what the hell is going on.

Nathalie and I bought some stretchy tights in revolting prison grey to wear under our jeans while Julian purchased a pair of white long-johns and a high-button vest with long sleeves and when we returned to the villa, he put them on and wandered around imitating Lee Marvin singing in a deep husky voice *"I was bo-orn under a wandrin' star"* much to our amusement. He was never cold even on the windiest days when helping Mikalis in some project while we stayed indoors. I asked a visiting friend from the UK to bring some long-sleeved spencers from Marks and Spencer of course for Nathalie and me, and with these under our new Cretan pullovers we kept beautifully warm. We also purchased a pair of rubber boots for wet weather and I treated myself to a pair of black suede ankle boots; something I have hankered after for twenty years but could never afford in Australia — these were made in Spain.

Knitwear in Crete and elsewhere in Greece is of excellent quality and design. The Greek sense of colour is superb; perhaps it is because they are surrounded by a landscape full of natural colours and tones whether they be the maize, golden-brown and olive shades of summer with the varying sea blues and greens, or the mauves, dove and steely greys of winter. The middle-class women dress most elegantly with well-cut jackets over jumpers of wonderfully blended shades of greens and greys, navy and lime, indigo and scarlet. The men are even more beautifully turned out and generally better-looking with their leather jackets and well-cut pants; even the shepherds wear ex-army stock of good quality jodhpurs and overcoats in complementary tones of khaki, taupe and green. It does help to have good bone structure and often pale grey or blue eyes from way back.

*

At the end of January I went to the Police Station to find the doors and windows closed; the building was deserted. Puzzled and feeling slightly disorientated I walked around and peered into their favourite haunt — a pastry shop that sells the most delectable *spanakopitas,* spinach and cheese pies, *tiropitas,* cheese pies, and *bougatsas,* layers of pastry filled with vanilla custard and sprinkled with cinnamon, served hot and cut into squares. But not a sign of well-filled blue uniformed men lounging about; and no police cars or motorbikes. Gone. The woman in the pastry shop told me they were in the process of moving the office; they had been thrown out as the landlord had decided to turn the entire block into two apartments for his two rather plain daughters as a dowry. The new police station would open in a week. Maybe. It was downtown on the road into Agios Nikolaos she said, or maybe not.

"How the hell can a town function without its Tourist and Aliens' Police for an entire week?"

I asked Yiannis in the square one morning. He was on his motorbike dashing to the bus station where he worked at the ticket office when not driving his father's bus; helping at the villas or organising the supermarket that he also ran in the summer; it closed during the winter.

"It is out of season now. Nobody needs them!" he replied.

"Except me," I said wryly.

"And I bet they lose my papers in the move." Jokingly. But as I spoke I thought that many a true word was spoken in jest.

"*If* the papers have arrived!" Yiannis said, the wisdom of the past months echoing in his voice.

The new police station when I found it, was spick and span and a great improvement on the old one but the move had not markedly changed Manolis' attitude to me. He looked up and then away again when I approached his new office.

'Oh Lord,' I thought.

'Here we go again, bring out the ice-breaker, engines full steam ahead!' as I ignored the shuttered look in his eyes and breezed in, smiling expectantly hand out-stretched. I still felt like Brown Owl.

"Kalimera," I gushed following my usual pattern in Greek naturally.

"Have the papers arrived yet Kirie Manoli?"

Finally he looked up at me in silence. Wonder upon wonder, my papers and the blue resident's card had arrived from Athens; he opened my file which was on his desk and showed it to me but, he said heavily, he could not give me the card because they had lost the original contract between the Greek National Tourist Organisation and Villa Olga's owner, which is in Marika's name for obvious reasons. I reeled back in disbelief — *they* had lost the contract therefore I could not have my resident's card? The logic escaped me. For a nation that surely invented logical thinking, there is little of it practised by today's Greeks in official positions.

"I *must* have my residency," I stated firmly, determined to make a stand.

"It has been issued by Athens and you may not keep it. It belongs to me doesn't it?" I smiled, or was it a grimace?

He mumbled something about keeping his records straight and that without the contract they were incomplete. He was immovable and when he saw my expression he got up and left the office. The interview was definitely over. I staggered down the steps and rode home in a fury to yet another cup of soothing *Dictamo,* mountain tea; this last hold-up was too much to put up with and I wondered if I was mad to continue with this quest to remain here against seemingly insurmountable odds. I was fast running out of steam and optimism.

Predictably, as dawn came with it came my high spirits and determination to succeed so we all went to Heraklion to see our friend the British Vice-Consul and gave her our story; this was not the first time we had raced to her for help and advice. She rang the head of the Aliens' Police in Heraklion, Manolis — yes another one — whom she said was efficient and helpful and he said he would speak to our man, but that he had no jurisdiction over him at all and could only ask the reasons for the hold-up.

Back to Agios Nikolaos and Manolis who was politer than usual but remained adamant. No contract meant no blue card. I was at my most persuasive I thought. I would get a photocopy of the old contract from the G.N.T.O. in Heraklion who issued all contracts. That would be no good he said because they all expired on the thirty-first of December, which was true, so I would have to get a new contract.

"But," I argued," they don't *issue* them until June of this year." Also true.

He knew this and looked at me with an expression that read, "That's your problem, ducky — not mine."
I stormed out, regrettably showing my frustration yet again and seriously considering a sit-in, but it was cold in his office and I was not quite ready to take such drastic measures. Once again we drove to Heraklion and the Greek National Tourist Organisation where we found the most efficient and pleasant people who spoke excellent English and seemed anxious to help. What a relief. They brought my file to the front desk within seconds of our arrival and listened to my problem. They thought a photocopy would do, so with a stamped and signed photocopy of the last contract, we returned triumphantly to Manolis. I handed him the copy feeling somewhat less confident as I saw his dark, disinterested eyes glaring at me as he brushed it aside. He needed *this year's* contract. I could not face another cup of mountain tea so Julian and I resorted to a stiff vodka and fresh orange juice while we mulled over the stalemate. We phoned the G.N.T.O. in Heraklion and told them we required a new contract for this year.

The man was sorry but the forms were not even printed so he was unable to give me his written permission for this year's contract.

Following several more vodkas and discussion we felt better and began to think laterally which my son invariably advises me to do if a little hazily. It appeared that Villa Olga as well as all the other villas on Crete, were being operated illegally since *all* the contracts expired on the thirty-first of December and the new ones were not issued until June. Perhaps if I put this quite sobering fact down in a letter to the G.N.T.O. they might find their way to giving me some form of permission to cover that period. It was definitely worth a try so I rang my friend in Heraklion and put this to him, adding,

"As I understand it, all the villas in Crete are now operating without a valid contract and will be until mid-June this year. Is not this so?"

A long silence and a slight cough followed.

"Yes, I suppose this is true."

I like to believe this had never struck him before. To cut an exceedingly long story short, I wrote a polite letter to the G.N.T.O. pointing this out and asking for something *in writing* permitting me to continue running Villa Olga until the new contracts were available. I received a reply — wonders will never cease — and a phone call saying he had sent the same letter to Manolis and that now the problem would be solved.

"Seeing is believing!" we said to one another and promptly forgot about the whole affair.

"After all this is Greece!" was becoming our stock phrase.

However, we misjudged them. Everything *was* all right. Manolis contacted me via Yiannis, gave me my blue card and my five-year residency and we parted quite amicably after another firm handshake. He even greets me in the street when we meet which he has never done before.

*

Drinking while on vacation seems almost mandatory and many unsuspecting visitors have discovered that it is easy — and cheap —

to become inebriated in Greece. Spirits are seldom measured; a 'tot' is seldom heard of and you are invariably poured a double whether you want one or not. I recall one of my most amusing experiences was with my teetotaller friend Anne with whom I used to work in Canberra, who was visiting me. It was lunchtime in Lion's Square in Heraklion. I ordered a gin and tonic and a fresh orange juice for her as we sat and watched the world go by beneath a shady awning. As usual there was more gin than tonic so I bought an extra bottle of tonic and sipped quietly, enjoying the sharp coolness of the drink and catching up with Anne. Well after two she asked where we were going to eat, she was hungry. I had my eye on a rather shoddy but very popular taverna across the road — we were not going to eat in the square as it was full of tourists and the menus and prices were adjusted to their palette, not mine.

"Let's go across to that place — it's always full of locals so I know the food must be good," I said brightly, feeling slightly fuzzy in the head, adding, "I'm starving too, haven't eaten since about seven this morning."

I registered this must be the reason the alcohol had gone to my head. "I need food badly." So we stood up. Then I sat down again. Stood up more slowly. Anne looked at me quizzically.

"Are you OK?" I sat down again my head spinning. "Yes I'm fine provided I don't have to walk anywhere, sorry but we'll have to eat here!"

So we ate their inferior quality food, I ask you rice and *peas?* at exorbitant prices and I vowed never to have a Cretan gin and tonic on an empty stomach again.

CHAPTER FIFTEEN

GREEK EASTER
A draconian ruse

The summer colours of rust, maize and olive dominate the land once again; where the contours of the island were softened and splashed with lush green clover so thick and moist that it squeaked underfoot, now the harsh beauty of the hot sun tones have replaced the pastel shades and unrelenting hard red clay lies beneath the olive groves where the black-eyed lambs gambolled and the ewes grazed beneath our villas, the bored goats are once more tethered to the trees flanking the villas, much to the delight of the new batch of kittens that have discovered them. They make little sallies from the safety of their hidey-hole then scamper back, tails a-bristle and ears flat, enchanting creatures whose capricious behaviour is fast ageing their patient mother who lies in the shade, tail swishing as she observes their skittish games.

The winter rains virtually failed and the talk is of a serious water shortage. Our supply is cut off at the mains every night and on two occasions when the villas have been full we have run out of mains water — but Mikalis is wily and he has a secret underground reservoir beneath Villa Seven and he switches on this extra supply when things are getting serious. I can remember thinking one night as I lay in my little villa at the bottom of the slope listening to the howling gale and heavy rainfall, that I hoped Mikalis had built up the walls of his reservoir properly or one of these days I would end up in the bay if it overflowed. So far so good.

I water the garden tentatively as does Mikalis and on the radio, we hear frequent broadcasts warning the population of the need to conserve water. I do admire the concern shown by the locals for the well-being of their island — the lack of rain and unusual early heat is on everyone's lips and on the mainland the problem is even greater as the reservoirs are running dangerously low already and summer and the tourist season have barely begun. It is feared that Athens will run out of water completely before the December rains.

I spoke to a blue-eyed German couple who sell the most beautiful vegetables at the Wednesday market. They look like leftover hippies from the sixties; she dresses like a gypsy in gay feminine skirts and soft blouses and sports an old-fashioned hat, but her eyes are ice-hard and her mouth thin and bitter. He on the other hand, is rather attractive, bearded and gentle with sad eyes; he told me they were already seriously affected by the water shortage and might go out of business.

Our fruit trees however have had sufficient rain to bear abundant crops; we have eaten sweet loquats until we can eat no more, there is only a little yellow flesh surrounding the glossy brown seeds but it is delectable; apricots, sun-flushed and softening are beginning to fall to the ground. The tree is so prolific. I have made apricot jam that sells well in my little shop together with the bitter marmalade that I have to say without modesty, is unbeatable and so simple to make. The cherry tree had a small crop that Mikalis picked in our absence one evening; I was somewhat surprised as he is normally so generous and we share everything. My son says it is his tree after all — and the crop was small. I guess he is right but it rankles.

*

Amanda my middle daughter and her partner Jeremy arrived from Sydney at the end of February and instantly fell in love with Villa Olga — a familiar refrain. She has taken over the vegetable garden from Nathalie who is mostly in town and her cabbages and tomatoes are standing strong and tall; she can be found any time of the day squatting down, her long blonde hair falling to her shoulders communing with her vegetables. Amanda once had ambitions of being a pianist with flute as a second instrument and throughout her childhood practised with astonishing diligence, winning a piano scholarship from the Director of the Canberra School of Music. But I left her with the family and her father to visit my mother in England during which time she fell in love and threw music away for a while. Now in her mid-twenties, she has come to Crete for a year with her partner and Jenny, a guitarist with whom she played duets in Canberra, has just arrived. The duo has already been booked for the season to play in up-market hotels in Agios Nikolaos and Elounda and for recitals organised by the Agios Nikolaos Music Society and there is rumour of a live radio broadcast. Who would have thought that music would return to her life in Crete — albeit on flute not piano?

Golden-skinned Francesca who was here for the first six months of last year and vowed to return this year has been unable to save enough money but will visit for a month's holiday in October. Living in Sydney with its spiralling costs, car repairs and a Burmese cat with bad teeth have wreaked havoc on her plans; meanwhile, she has been a marvellous ambassador for Villa Olga and has put in some Spartan work publicising our villas amongst friends and business acquaintances in Australia. Strange how things turn out. She was always going to be a ballet dancer and I see her as a fairy child, dancing with joy on the lawn in her miniature tutu, daisies in her hair and holding a daisy chain as she practises her solo ballet steps. Her hobby now is choreography — so she is still in touch with dance — her first love.

And Philippa is twenty-three tomorrow; living and working as a violinist in Sydney sometimes in 'my' old orchestra much to my delight, playing operatic and ballet works. One of my most precious memories is of her with a fractured wrist in plaster, trying out her first Chinese-made violin at the age of six and insisting on attending a holiday camp for young string players, where she excelled despite the handicap. Always I find it hard to hear a violin without wanting to share it with her. And always I weep quietly. It is the same with the piano. In my mind's eye I can still see the young Amanda playing with such delicacy and sensitivity and I cannot help wishing she had not abandoned her chosen path with the piano. But we make our choices. No one makes them for us.

And my son, my strong and silent son. Always there, humorous and a bit secretive but then men often are I tell myself — and Nathalie still enjoying her days in Agios Nikolaos teaching her delightful shy Cretan children.

*

As I write I am looking over the bay that lies so far below me through the flowering pomegranate and the bright orange trumpet flower.

There is a solitary white sail on the cobalt sea and the Thripte Mountains are clear and perfectly defined against a bleached sky. I feel a bit like that yacht at the moment, being taken this way and that by the wind having some but not total control over the future. Is there such a thing as a future or has everything happened before and are we just running the reel of life's film again to see what it was like, to experience the intense pleasure and pain — the highs and the lows? If I tried could I *remember* what is going to happen in say, six months? Or in six years? And do I want to? The answer is definitely, "No!"

*

In April both Europa and Tit-Bits had kittens a few days apart. Julian and Nathalie were in France at the time and Jeremy and I had to determine which kittens to keep and which to dispose of. Amanda could not bear to be involved and kept well away; this painful and dreadful task upset us for days but we could not have ten kittens at Villa Olga and Mikalis refused point-blank to share the high cost of neutering. He waved his hand angrily in the air and said that cars on the road and poison from the village would dispose of them soon enough. He's right about the cars — we lost delightful Purring Pumpkin during the winter and missed her greatly. Jeremy and I decided to allow each cat one kitten and I named Europa's dark grey male tabby kitten "Geronimo" after Jeremy for being so courageous, and Tit-Bits' white and tabby-splashed kitten "Oedipus" as we had a feeling he would be faced with the riddle of which female he belonged to as they shared one another's kittens.

In fact 'the girls' as the two sisters are now called and their shared kittens are the prettiest sight I have yet to see in the animal world. They have nested in a cupboard and have a babysitting arrangement whereby when one goes out hunting the other takes over both kittens, feeding and cleaning and generally mothering. Then they swap places and the kittens go automatically to the other female. Yet when the sisters are together, the kittens feed only from their real mothers. For some reason, the girls decided their brother Jupiter to be *persona non grata* and chased him off the property. He visited tentatively now and then, befuddled at the un-sisterly behaviour but they were so vicious and aggressive he gave up and we have not seen him for a while. I do miss him because he always met us when we came home and would trot along by our heels up the terraces on his big ungainly paws purring and curling round our feet with sheer joy at our presence. Last year before she left for Australia Francesca christened him Paddle-Paws which suited him well.

Following the arrival of the kittens the girls also decided that Crosspatch, a miniature tortoiseshell with a down-turned mouth that adopted us during the winter, was no longer welcome and she was summarily pursued across the vacant lot beside the villas and eventually disappeared. Surprisingly though they permitted Tiger Tim to remain though they were hostile and spat and hissed at him whenever he was in sight — so by degrees the cat population has been decreased to five and that is how it stands at the moment.

*

Easter or *Pascha* as it is called in Greece was a time of sheer disappointment and frustration for me. Last year I had a recurring bout of what seemed like glandular fever that went on for months; then I was clear of symptoms for a while until February this year when back came the aching limbs, sore throat, throbbing and swollen glands and overwhelming fatigue. Over Easter, I felt so ill that I missed the celebrations I had been so longing to experience though I am not a church-goer and belong to no religion except for my style of what might be called Buddhism. The family told me all about the solemn ceremony led by richly robed church dignitaries and the carrying of Christ's coffin all around the town to the port; the church services; the spectacular burning of Judas Iscariot's body over the lake and the Cretans leaving the various churches with their lit candles endeavouring to get them home alight to ensure good fortune for the rest of the year; and at midnight the somewhat terrifying fireworks over the lake and the huge explosives that were thrown into the water — I wondered about the fish — as the Cretans proclaimed

Christos Amnisos, Christ is risen; after which they went to their homes to eat various unmentionable delicacies like cooked entrails.

I had intended to dye eggs and decorate the villa with flowers but had insufficient energy or interest to do anything at all. The locals bake a large round loaf with a dyed red egg in the centre, but there were no hot cross buns and I did miss them. Habit dies hard.

I did pass by the Byzantine church off the square in Agios Nikolaos with its richly decorated interior in maroon and gold and the scent of incense. It was full to bursting and through the narrow wooden doorway came the most glorious plainsong chanting as old as time — thick with earnest male voices. So moving. I could have stood there all evening but for my aching bones and as I climbed back into my solitary bed I did think that if God had any decency at all he'd have made sure that I was at least well enough to enjoy my first Greek Easter.

I felt better on Easter Sunday and we went to a South-African Greek couple's villa for lamb on the spit. Stavros and his French girlfriend had just had a baby, a little girl and the extended family was there en masse. It was a happy day though I found the constant and loud presence of the television somewhat disconcerting. Everyone was invited to have a go at turning the spit handle that was kept in constant motion for about five hours, thirsty work and gallons of wine and beer were consumed as the afternoon wore on. Finally at about four, we had a fabulous meal when the succulent lamb garnished with lemon juice and oregano was carved, accompanied by salads and potatoes followed by huge bowls of mixed fresh fruit. Entertainment was provided by an impromptu concert with Amanda on flute and Jenny on guitar and we finally staggered home full of good cheer. Even my glands felt better.

*

The villas have been full for many weeks now since early April which is gratifying and long may it last though it is tiring work. If anyone thinks running six villas is an easy way to make a living they should come and join us for a few weeks when we are full. Not only do we have to clean the vacated villas and leave them absolutely spotless and as if no one has ever occupied them — but we deliver and collect the linen from an industrial laundry twice a week, a drive of about sixteen kilometres because they refuse to deliver; the gas bottles for the stoves are constantly in need of replenishment; shopping for the family and extended family and friends plus keeping our shop supplied and the pool has to be kept clean; eight terraces of garden to be watered and weeded that takes hours and of course, planting new flowers not to mention all the cooking for my hungry family though of course I have plenty of help.

Keeping the clients happy and well informed about the island takes all our time and we often dine out with them; this is obviously most agreeable, but means a late night with less sleep and we start very early almost before sun-up each day.

What I do enjoy for the first time in my life is everyday cooking and trying out new Cretan dishes with appreciative family and friends. I have never really experienced the art of cooking before, mainly because I had an African *mpishi,* cook, until I came to Australia in 1962. To prepare myself for the move six months before leaving, I sadly and regretfully terminated the cook's position and taught myself the culinary arts, recipe book in hand on a wood stove in a soot-blackened kitchen in soaring temperatures. I lost a stone in weight which was a welcome side effect but I am not sure what that said about my cooking. Now I revel in going to the weekly market and experimenting with all the inviting fresh produce and new tastes and flavours. I am even thinking of writing a special 'Valerie's Cookbook', I am so thrilled with everything culinary for the first time in my life — and I am fifty-five, so more than halfway through but will I ever find the time to write anything at all I begin to wonder? My motto has always been:

Nulla dies sine linea — No day without a single line.
No day without something done.

And that is all well and good *if* one can find the time!

*

Our days have taken on a summer pattern. Last year we leapt onto our scooters and spent a few glorious hours at The Rock where a deep and refreshing dive to the dark cool depth would restore my equilibrium, vanquish my anxieties and give me energy. Then, lying on the warm sloping rocks with my family and occasionally friends from abroad we would thrash out some of the problems that had beset us — and often solve them with panache and insight as we relaxed. Nowadays the alternative is a swim in the pool in the afternoons and a rest in the shade of the pistachio trees, but it is not quite the same. I need our Rock and the far line of the horizon —I have always felt it gives me a perspective on life and even on the day's activities that results in a calming of the nervous system. It has always been thus. I virtually grew up swimming in the warmth of the Indian Ocean off Magagoni beach in Dar es Salaam — although I was sent up-country to boarding school at the age of seven far, far from the gentle embrace of the coastal waters. Being by the sea and swimming with and observing the intriguing antics of the few octopuses, the bobbing head of an occasional turtle, the schools of darting fish and of course after the swim, lying on The Rock and seeing the horizon always restores my super-charged enthusiasm. It gives all of us the real reason we fled our lives in Australia and headed north and for me only Crete would do. Everything about our afternoon's escapades would forever be magical, unforgettable and precious.

*

Perhaps being born an Aquarian has something to do with my need to be near water, more precisely by the sea, although curiously this is an Air sign and not a Water sign. The following unravels the puzzle if one asks the question:

Why is Aquarius known as the Water Bearer? The answer is:

The Greek astronomer Ptolemy in the second century recorded Aquarius. It is a constellation of the Zodiac and means 'cup or water bearer' in Latin and is one of the oldest constellations documented.

They say Aquarians have a certain inner strength. They know all energy comes from within and only that can take away whatever the pain. The power is theirs and this they know.

*

In April this year, we had guests keen to swim but were surprised to find how icy cold the sea was. Had the pool been filled the same complaint would have been voiced.

"Too cold, it's too cold!" They cried as they shivered after a dip in the sea, the water does not warm up until the end of May and not always then. Later, once the swimming pool was completed, it became a great attraction and swimming was a joy both in the sea and the pool. Some of our guests declined the offer of a lift to one of the beaches choosing instead, to loll around the pool, next to our small shop with cool drinks and their villas up a few steps, so close and convenient.

"We love the view of the bay and the mountains it is perfect and the chaises-longues are so comfortable plus the water is not salty! We don't find salt water comfortable on our skins!" said the pale couple from the north as they hailed their preferences.

*

There have been a lot of comings and goings with Julian and Jeremy working for an electrician called Nikos; the thought amuses me because my son is green-red colour-blind and I wonder how he will fare. They leave for work on their scooters at seven and return in the late afternoon quite worn out, hurl themselves into the pool then fall asleep sometimes for hours on end. At six-thirty sharp Amanda and Jenny go to town dressed up in their glad rags on the boys' two scooters with their flute and guitar strapped on their backs; they play bright and happy melodies for several hours then eat at the hotel where they have been performing. We have our meal and sometimes meet them in the port for a drink when they have finished; it is still daylight and the town is just warming up. It reaches the boil at about midnight and stragglers find their weary way home as dawn comes more often than not.

As for me, I occasionally join in and have a fantastic time but mostly stay at home to read or see if there is a good late film on television, despite the half-hour interruption — however by evening I sometimes begin to feel my age which is perhaps not surprising. Our days start very early and apart from the afternoon break we all seem to work non-stop until night falls. What I find rewarding is living so close to my family again whereas in Sydney we were all working and did not often find the time to get together. I was never free at night, opera and ballet orchestral management six nights a week was my 'entertainment' and I did love it.

Here we determine how our days pan out, more or less depending on the arrivals and departures of guests and the midnight flights that bring them in and carry away those who were occupying the villas. Living the Greek way of life with its happy and carefree attitudes and the belief that life is for living and not only for working, has changed our mindsets and being closely surrounded by the warmth of other human beings and having the time to communicate with everyone is what life is all about.

*

It was the smell of doughnuts that did it. Amanda and I were shopping in the square in Agios Nikolaos which isn't a square at all but a roundabout with a hedge full of cigarette butts and ice-cream papers, four massive date palms and a statue. The ubiquitous νεραντζιά, *nerantzia* trees produce the bitter Seville oranges that we use for our marmalade, also grow within the roundabout and bear bright glowing fruit in the winter. They make the best marmalade; — but this was summer and the height of the tourist season and we were heading towards Buttercup and thinking of returning to the villas for a mid-morning coffee when we passed Yiannis' *kafenion* with its tables and chairs beneath bright awnings. He saw us from inside and came rushing out, his rotund figure bursting with energy. Today he decided to speak English. It depended on his mood as to whether he spoke Greek or English and this had an interesting effect on the British tourists who had perhaps, on the previous day, heard him speak perfect English. And on the next, it would be a stream of incomprehensible Greek spoken at double the speed. Quite a feat in itself. His brown eyes would crease with amusement as he watched their confusion, but he would stick to his guns and not alter the language of the day.

"Where are you going girls?" he asked with that slightly bossy manner often used by Greek males the world over when speaking to the opposite sex.

"We've been shopping and now we're going home," replied my slender daughter, long-legged, brown and beautiful with her hair bleached almost white by the sun,

"And we are *not* coming to have a doughnut with you!" Giggling and issuing a challenge no self-respecting Greek male could ignore.

"Why not?" He demanded, drawing his brows together. "Today they might be free. You never know come and sit down,"

And he pulled two plastic chairs out for us and disengaged my arm from the parcel I was holding. We looked at each other realising that all was lost — we invariably ended up at Yiannis' place for either doughnuts or cheese pies with a *café frappé.*

"Oh all right." We feigned reluctance adding,

"But they'd better be free!"

They weren't of course but they might have been as Crete is still a cheap country despite gradually rising costs. We sipped our frothy iced coffee, drank cold water and covered ourselves with icing sugar as we waded through the delectable and outsized doughnuts.

On our way back along the winding road overlooking the Bay of Mirabello, I said smugly,

"Well at least we didn't pick up a parking fine this time."

We had a collection of parking tickets incurred by Julian and me in the tray of the car; parking in high season is impossible in the town and it seemed that wherever Julian or I left Buttercup we would collect yet another parking ticket which we never attempted to pay. I knew that the locals never paid parking fines and as I considered our family to be 'locals' I didn't see why we should front up with our Anglo-Saxon sense of propriety and correctness, to cough up sums of money when nobody else did. I had my five-year residency and had been there over a year and what could be more local than that? I also knew there was no follow-up as it was all too hard in the season with hundreds — thousands — of tourists' vehicles coming and going every few days. Having said that I occasionally felt a bit guilty as I broke the law again and again, and on that particular morning I had parked where I was convinced it was legal — next to a new taxi sign — I moved in as another car reversed out, assuming it was legally parked.

We hauled our shopping bags up the terraces, unpacked in the cool of the villa and went about our various tasks after a refreshing swim in the pool; villa cleaning, stocking the shop, skimming the pool of the myriad wasps and insects attracted by the prolific fruit trees. All pleasant and non-stressful work. But hot. Later — lunch on our terrace — *paximathia* salad and of course a little Cretan rosé with a clink of ice then siesta, a good book and a half-hour nap while the cicadas shrieked totally ignoring the noise ban during siesta which is between two and five p.m. Another dip in the pool and we thought a trip to the windmills above Elounda would be fun before the evening took over. Down to Buttercup. To our astonishment there were no number plates. I looked around thinking for a wild moment that they must have fallen off and might be on the ground; how stupid one can be momentarily, but of course they were not on the ground.

"Where *can* they be? Someone's stolen them — but why? To put on a stolen car maybe?"

We put forward all sorts of hypotheses but none seemed to make any sense. Finally as always when in doubt — phone Yiannis. He always knows what to do.

"Someone has stolen our number plates, Yianni. What can we do?" we bleated over the phone.

He laughed; his voice loud over the background din of the bus station.

"Hah! You parked in a bad place!" he shouted — Greeks invariably shout down the phone, "and the police they have taken your number plates."

"The *police*?" I echoed incredulously.

"The police have taken my number plates? But why?"

"You are parking in a bad place," and he guffawed, "so you must to pay a fine for a change. You have to go and buy them back."

I gulped. Oh God — would we have to pay *all* the accumulated fines I wondered? I knew they were expensive — about forty Australian dollars a time I had been told.

"I will to go with Julian tomorrow," yelled Yiannis, breaking into Greek as he answered my queries.

"Tell him he must to come with me and we will get the number plates," and he laughed again and I heard him telling the clerks at the information desk about the *xenia,* foreigners, who had finally got caught by the police. I told my son when he returned from town and he paled visibly.

"Oh, God," he echoed my thoughts, "will we have to pay them all?"

Optimistically I said, "I wouldn't think so. They have no computers you know and can't follow through."

"I hope you're right," he replied fervently.

"Me too!" As I handed him a wad of notes with which to purchase back our number plates.

Next day he went with Yiannis to the police station, paid the single fine and collected the number plates; no mention was made of any of the other parking tickets and he came home mightily relieved. We thought seriously of welding on the number plates and had noticed that many of the local cars had done just that — now we knew the reason.

A little while later I double-parked Buttercup by the post office while Amanda dashed in to post some letters. At the top of the steep road I watched two policemen, smart in their blue uniforms, systematically removing the number plates with their spanners from the vehicles parked illegally down to the port. They had their work cut out for them — we moved on before they reached us!

CHAPTER SIXTEEN

WE ARE FILM EXTRAS
The games Mikalis and I play

"They're advertising for extras in a French film on board a luxury cruiser in the bay," announced Andy, a tall Australian staying at Villa Olga.

"Anybody interested? They're paying as well!" Might be fun!

We responded with alacrity and in record time we were in Agios Nikolaos at the travel agency that was handling recruitment for the film. They told us that we were to wear our own cocktail outfits since there was no wardrobe supplied for casuals. I was not impressed. We had to be on the Greek cruise ship called *Narcissus,* for the purpose of the film, by eight the next morning; we would be fed and paid forty Australian dollars a day. Unfortunately, Amanda and Jenny were unable to take part as their musical activities in hotel dining rooms started too early each evening; Jeremy — who had grown a beard — would be required for the engine-room scene later on, but for some reason he was never called.

Julian, Andy and I plus a young couple also from Villa Olga boarded the moored ship in the cool of the morning feeling somewhat ridiculous dressed up in fancy cocktail garb at that time of the morning. There were about twenty extras from various walks of life; a few residents like us and holiday-makers all intrigued to be part of a film which was called *La Femme Fardée,* The Painted Lady, based on a novel by Françoise Sagan starring Jeanne Moreau and Alain Delon and several other well-known actors. Disappointingly, both Moreau and Delon had done their parts in Athens and left — I should like to have seen them in the flesh so to speak. The main characters were a gorgeous Italian actress as the painted lady and her husband who, with his smouldering eyes and Roman profile held the rapt attention of every woman on the ship — and some of the men I noticed. He was a hunk!

We gathered on the stern deck where a long bar decorated with blue and white paper flowers and streamers held champagne glasses with coloured water and plates of cardboard or plastic *hors d'oeuvres.* I was coupled with a middle-aged Hollander who had come aboard just for fun and when the waiter who was one of the extras came round with the appetizers, he took one and put it in his mouth and almost choked as someone shouted,

"You can't eat these, they're plastic props!"

The poor man was covered with confusion and said in explanation as he choked, "But I'm starving!"

We were handed blue and white balloons on long strings and champagne glasses filled with some liquid which my partner did not attempt to taste and instructed to, "Look 'appy!" by the French director.

"You are at a cocktail party on a smart boat. Look 'appy!"

This we tried to do but after two hours in the extreme heat, walking to and fro doing take after take we began to flag. It was also quite hazardous as we kept tripping over the rails of *the dolly*, the moving camera trolley and the miles of cable and lighting wires that lay all over the deck, attached to cameramen and soundmen who were lying at strange angles — presumably to get interesting shots; not to mention the wandering waiters with their trays of non-drinks. The balloons became a source of irritation as they got caught in my hair and my handbag and I allowed two of mine to blow away. After all, who in their right minds would hold a couple of balloons at a cocktail party for heaven's sake? But they were instantly replaced. We were also given handfuls of confetti at intervals but never told exactly when to throw it.

There was a certain lack of direction and I considered offering myself as a continuity girl as no one seemed to be totally in charge. One of the scenes involves a quarrel where the jealous husband knocks a champagne glass out of his inebriated wife's hand. After the initial *fifteen* dry runs using a plastic mug, shooting began with a genuine champagne glass; the cameras began to roll — and roll — and roll. Each time the glass splintered on the wooden deck its contents had to be dried with a hair drier and the angry scene re-enacted yet again while we did our best to look elegant and lively with aching feet and sweaty brows. Luckily the Dutchman and I were in the background and could relax a bit, but Julian was partnered with a pretty young woman from Villa Olga and they were in the front row in the direct line of the camera and would certainly have been in every shot taken.

"Fame at last!" My son grinned at me as we watched the quarrelling couple for the hundredth time.

Finally as frayed nerves had reached a fever pitch the catch-cry "*Lili*" was called out. This word for some reason meant the shoot had been successful. A cheer went up and we trooped down to the cool saloon and lunched gratefully, enjoying fine French wines to the full. Following the meal the young sprawled across the couches and chairs like discarded puppets and slept. Why is it that young people are so much more tired than their elders — we were weary but not exhausted.

*

The ship was atrociously appointed. Luxurious it was not; with clashing carpets and wallpaper, dirty windows and grubby upholstery it reminded me of those beach houses where all the left-over scraps of carpet, curtaining and furniture not used in 'the main house' are utilised with the resultant clash of colour and design. But at a beach house, it doesn't matter. However we were well fed even if the last in the queue got short rations; tea, coffee and soft drinks were available the entire day with occasional sandwiches and it was air-conditioned. The mixture of cultures and language was interesting; the French film crew had their Greek counterparts and they worked well together, not much English was spoken and the phrase '*Repetez s'il vous plait;* as we did take after take became a familiar call. The director was surprisingly good-natured considering that he and the film crew and cast had been aboard the *Narcissus* for six weeks since they started shooting in Athens prior to coming to Crete. Only the 'bit' actors and actresses showed any sign of hostility towards one another and for some, it had obviously been a long six weeks. The 'permanents' as they were called were a rum lot, mainly Greek-Americans who had joined the ship in Athens to relieve the boredom of being rich. One voluptuous and talkative woman gave me graphic details of her multi-coloured colostomy bag and her three ex-husbands in the same brandy-soaked breath and displayed an inordinate amount of curiosity about me and my family as I became progressively more tight-lipped.

On several occasions I was collared by an anorexic 'bit' actress with glazed eyes and her face falling apart at the seams as she teetered around on dangerously high heels; within moments she told me that she had been booked for the main part in the film but 'that bitch' had got to the producer first. No doubt the casting was done on the couch as is reputedly often the case. I observed the general movement by the other actors to other parts of the deck when she appeared — obviously one to be avoided.

And the others; a beautiful Botticelli girl with a skin of white marble and an abundance of curling red hair; a rangy Dutchman with secretive body language and ill-fitting false teeth; a New Zealand girl made up in 'Dynasty' style with her thick blonde hair in plaits around her head.

There were several noisy Australians who kept everyone awake during the short siesta and made themselves thoroughly unpopular with the cast and camera crew. Their comments evoked raucous mirth amongst themselves but none from anyone else; the tired and surly Englishman who read his newspaper and spoke to no one, obviously wishing it was all over — but then why did he come? And the rest:

two large-boned Hollanders, one of whom ate the prop and was my partner who came just for the experience.

the mandatory English female — middle-aged and fast-fading north countrywoman who boasted that she had come to Crete for the sole and loudly stated purpose of finding a man — any man but preferably one of those sexy smouldering Cretan boys;

an inebriated and loud Cockney in her late sixties who was surprisingly erudite and sensitive as we discussed spiritualism and Buddhism with fervour. She was a lonely and sad soul; the tall and elegantly dressed couple who looked like diplomats and I discovered were exactly that; "Just doing it for kicks," the woman said laconically, tossing back her auburn hair, diamonds catching the sun. Certainly they would have been well-rehearsed in what was expected at an up-market cocktail party;

the cigar-smoking short and balding tycoon, a Londoner who had been running strip joints and wanted to start one up in Elounda. Heaven forbid I thought and refused to discuss his proposed project or help him with his eagerly sought local information;

the tired body language and rusty voice of the local Cretan representative and the *croupier*, a charming man.

One of the permanent actors was an eighty-one-year-old eccentric American-Greek from Houston who with long white hair, beard and sporting an outfit of shiny sequined white clothes was the spitting image of the Colonel Sanders' chicken advertisements on television — but was unimpressed when I mentioned the similarity. He became quite a nuisance as he insisted on following me around the ship — mind you he paid me the nicest compliments. His wife, bejewelled and gold-chained with her down-turned mouth and anxious eyes had every reason to be suspicious of her husband's fidelity, but she need not have worried about me. Before the shoot ended he insisted on giving me a signed book of his poems and in the following weeks somehow found out the Villa Olga phone number and rang me from Athens several times to try to arrange a rendezvous on one of the islands. He also begged me to visit Athens where he would take me to all the top nightclubs and I could meet all his friends. Weird, I thought and what about his wife? Rumour has it that it is customary if not mandatory for Greek husbands to have a mistress somewhere, as do most Mediterranean males I gather. I do recall thinking wryly that my age was certainly beginning to show if the only romantic interest I could evoke was from a man well past his 'used-by' date. But he was a quietly-spoken charmer nonetheless.

*

All the time our ship cruised gently around the blue bay with the barren Siteia mountains folding towards us and out to sea a glimpse of the far horizon. It would be a colourful film and very Greek in character — even if the characters were not all Greek.

*

On returning to the villas one evening after shooting I noticed yet another of my precious succulents collected from the hillsides around the Milatos caves in the winter, had a heavy stone sitting on top of it. I lifted it up; the main stem was smashed in two. Another accidental killing by that old rogue Mikalis. He and I have had a running battle over my introduction to the terraces of this spectacular euphorbia that covers itself in brilliant greeny-yellow florets in mid-winter adding sorely needed colour to the wintry hillsides. When I challenged him he said it had a bad smell. I said only if you broke a branch off as he had just done to the one on the lowest terrace which was barren and needed shrubs and ground cover — and anyway, didn't he like the yellow flowers? He shrugged and grinned. Yes he liked the yellow flowers but he did not like the shrub. It had a bad odour! I had planted six rooted shoots and he systematically destroyed the lot either with a well-placed stone or by hauling the hose pipe across them, or by stepping on them.

"Right!" I said to myself. "I'll get my own back."

I had noticed that he had planted a variety of vegetables in between the new flower beds along the terraces — this was all fine and dandy but for the cabbages which grew to enormous proportions and outstripped all the flowering plants I was attempting to establish. Had he been a bit more careful when planting them, it might have worked but he was not the most vigilant gardener and each time he ventured into the borders he would step on my precious seedlings – and he was aware of this. We had established a small vegetable garden above the tiny courtyard behind Villa Two so gradually I removed his invasive vegetables and transplanted them into *our* vegetable garden where there was space for them to expand. He didn't notice for a long time until one morning I watched him arrive in his blue van and walk up the terraces shaking his head and mouthing what I knew to be the unmentionable 'm' word as he saw the bare patches between my flowers, where his vegetables had once stood. But neither of us said anything — just exchanged knowing looks and continued to do what we were doing. The family calls it 'our game'. Yet I believe he approved the transformation of the terraces which last summer were dry and baked and a source of continuous dust and dirt.

I recall him one morning watching Nathalie as she thrust a pick into the rock-hard surfaces and turned the soil over strongly, her brown arms glowing in the sun. She loved digging and preparing the beds for planting, something I was quite unable to do hampered as I was with my grafted spine. Now where the many terrace walls were unadorned we have planted a charming ground cover with brilliant shocking pink flowers that cascade down the stone walls, it is a variety of mesembryanthemum that in Australia is called oddly, Pigface. When Mikalis first saw it he drew his brows together and muttered something that I ignored as is my wont whenever he mutters something with a frown — but now I've noticed he has planted the odd cutting himself and is pleased with the results.

There is still one running battle that I am determined he won't win. It is to do with mulching. It seems that Cretans know nothing about mulching as I have put shallow-rooted ground covers around the many citrus trees to protect their roots from the blazing sun and to retain moisture I have swept leaves and uprooted weeds around the boles— but every time I have done this he has ripped out all the plants and swept away the mulch. I expect I shall have to admit defeat eventually as after all, they are his citrus trees not mine, I am just borrowing them for the time being and one certainly cannot teach an old Cretan dog new tricks and hope to win them all!

*

John, one of our Sydney friends who was visiting, offered to help with the evening meal; we would barbecue a chicken in the outside bread oven; the oven in the kitchen was so rusty that it barely heated up and anyway I think the boys felt like doing something different. The problem was that it had been raining and while the oven itself was dry — being an upturned clay pot of huge dimensions — the wood and kindling were damp. After endless attempts at getting the wood alight Jeremy suggested they use some lighter fuel, so he sprayed some onto the wood and threw in a match. Within a second there was an explosion like a cannon going off and a huge fireball flew out of the open oven door, propelling both Julian and Jeremy to the back of the courtyard.

John and I were in the kitchen and saw the flash and the terrifying sight of them being hurled backwards though I noticed Julian had managed to turn aside and escape the main fireball which caught Jeremy fair and square on his arms and the side of his face. The smell of burning hair and flesh, mostly Jeremy's, was awful and once we had ascertained they were not badly hurt my fear turned to anger and according to Julian — for I have forgotten this — I turned on them like a virago for being so bloody stupid. John tried to calm me down, but it took some time as I *do* remember that my knees did not stop shaking for the entire evening.

The incident in retrospect sounds amusing but it was not at the time; they could both have been badly burned, if not killed by the blast. I also carry the never-ending trauma of seeing Julian, six years of age, burned over two-thirds of his body in Far North Queensland when he ran across what he thought was a dump of sandy soil at the end of a friend's land by the Mossman sugar mills. He fell deep into the huge pile which beneath the top layer, was burning red-hot *bagasse*, the dry fibrous residue remaining after the extraction of juice from the crushed stalks of sugar cane, dumped there from the mills. We were staying with friends, both of whom were out at the time and it was a weekend; there was no one on duty when I rang for an ambulance initially and the long wait for help was a nightmare. This all whirled through my brain, reignited by the smell of burning flesh and hair and the expression in my son's eyes as they met mine briefly as he was propelled towards the wall at the end of the courtyard.

My subconscious retains the horror of the earlier experience from which he healed with barely a scar to show for his pain; my scars go deep and surface now and then and I feel sick with the memory.

*

When John first arrived in Crete we tried to persuade him to hire a scooter so that he could explore the island. The idea appalled him, and he responded with passion.

"No way am I going to be seen dead on one of those things!"

So we gave up. Later, following the arrival of Greg another Sydney friend, John allowed himself to be persuaded to at least have a trial run. Urged on by our vociferous encouragement and some practice he decided it was, after all a good idea, so one morning he and Greg headed for the hills; got lost somewhere and took a dirt road through a small and almost deserted village where they were attacked by a pack of aggressive dogs. They were compelled to lift their feet onto the handlebars and race through the village at great speed closely followed by the pack of barking, teeth-baring hounds, then to their dismay the track turned out to be a dead-end so they had to turn around, rev up and with feet on the handlebars roar *back* through the village and the waiting dogs their tongues hanging out, eyes blazing.

"More like wolves," remarked John with a grimace on his return home.

To add insult to injury the weather that had been sunny and warm when they set off had suddenly turned nasty, a heavy damp cloud enveloped them and the temperature dropped dramatically. They were frozen when they arrived back at the villas, but had managed to comfort themselves by having a succulent meal en route at a taverna in Itanos and entertained us with their droll and often humorous comments on the doubtful joys of exploring this part of the island.

CHAPTER SEVENTEEN

ON REFLECTION
We made the right choice

There is a wonderful ambience about life in Crete. Relaxed. Unhurried. No one ever seems to be in too much of a rush to stop and talk, sit and have a coffee or just stand at a street corner and chat for an hour. Time has a different meaning — there seems to be more of it and it has stretched to encompass the good things of life. All this is great for the holidaymaker but decidedly counter-productive if one is attempting to start a business. The roadside *kafenia* are filled with elderly Cretan men — this is not a woman's domain — drinking tiny white cups of thick Greek coffee or small glasses of ouzo as they discuss the events of the day whether it be politics —which is most likely now with Greece having had three elections in ten months — or the olive crop, the tourist trade and possibly the occasional bad behaviour of their handsome sons in the tourist season — and they are *so* handsome — with those long-legged blondes from the northern countries. The older men are invariably well dressed and take no notice of foreigners as they fiddle with their *komboloyia* or swing them round their little fingers. I have noticed with some amusement that although the young men have eschewed the use of worry beads per se, they nonetheless fiddle with their car or motorbike keys in the same manner; the need to fidget with something is apparent.

The elderly, both men and women give a sense of stability to this holiday port and thankfully many of the shops and tavernas have remained stubbornly Cretan with no attempt to titivate or modernise the premises. In grocery stores beneath faint light bulbs, the jumble of goods is piled high from floor to ceiling on shelves so thick with dust one has to blow it off before reading the faded labels — this makes shopping interesting if a bit time-consuming. But it is partly a social occasion anyway and greetings and gossip are the most important aspect of the visit — the purchases are of secondary importance. It has taken a while to become known in the town but now we are welcomed as residents and it gives me a warm glow — a sense of belonging in this popular destination of summer transients.

The restaurants tavernas and bars with their bright awnings and gaudy modern décor that sit around the harbour and the deep lake could be almost anywhere — but in the square and side streets one sees Agios Nikolaos and early Crete almost unchanged. One could only be in Greece for in their tavernas décor is non-existent — rickety wooden tables covered with plastic table-cloths or in some cases, butcher's paper; a blaring television probably heralding yet another game of football; plastic flowers thick with dust — but once inside the door one's senses are overwhelmed with the enticing aromas coming from the primitive kitchen where one is invited to choose the evening meal. This procedure is expected of any visitor and is welcomed by the proud cook, quite often a smiling middle-aged woman who will make one feel immediately at home as she assists in the difficult decisions to be made from the array of pulsating and inviting dishes on the stove top. Village wine is often questionable and sometimes positively undrinkable but one can purchase a good average Cretan wine for less than two English pounds or four Australian dollars per litre and a half — so who's complaining? The music, atmosphere and welcoming warmth in these often simple tavernas are so inviting that one never wants the evening to end. One is amongst friends.

*

We have run out of our homemade bitter marmalade both for our consumption and for our little shop on the premises, so on our trip to the weekly market we purchased grape-fruit, oranges, lemons and clementines that are the smallest variety of mandarin and orange. They are similar to tangerines but where tangerines have knobbly skins, clementines are smooth. We bought six of each, firm not over-ripe and of average size since we have only two large saucepans.

The other ingredient is white sugar and I can only judge how much by frequently tasting it during the last hour or so of the process. If I were making a batch just for the family I would prepare two of each of the four citrus fruit; sometimes three work just as well. I add half to three-quarters of a kilo of sugar and stir constantly which can become a bit of a bore, it seems to take so long to set although the pectin from the pips must be useful. A warning — it is too late once you have added too much sugar, it will no longer be a truly bitter marmalade which is the aim of the exercise!

The method for making my now 'famous' three or four-fruit bitter marmalade follows:

First I wash the fruit and prick the skins with a sharp knife, cover with water and simmer for well over an hour with the lid on until all the contents are soft and the liquid is reduced by half or less. I add boiling water to bring up the level so at least three-quarters of the contents remain covered. Then I leave it overnight or until it is cool enough to cut the fruit in half, squeeze out the juice and save the pips for their pectin content in a muslin bag of some kind; tie in a knot and boil with the fruit. I cut the peel and pulp into the thick chunky pieces we like best and return it all to the saucepan, adding a little more water depending on how much it has been reduced.

Let it boil gently possibly for an hour or more, with the lid off and keep stirring until it turns a golden-brown colour then add half the sugar and taste before adding more until the setting point is reached, taking care not to let it burn. Scoop off any froth on top. When it begins to congeal and sometimes it never congeals but still tastes good. For dark brown marmalade, let it caramelise briefly just when it begins to stick to the bottom of the pan, but do take care. The last thing is to let it cool slightly before bottling it in jars that have been sterilised with boiling water beforehand. We amuse ourselves by designing attractive labels of glowing golden oranges with dark green leaves for the bottles and a similar idea with sprigs of glossy olives for the many jars of our very own olive oil.

*

I often find it difficult to find time to jot down the day's activities in my journal but the need to record even the most insignificant detail is hard-wired into my brain. One day I might see my illustrated pieces already published in various travel publications, in book form which is eventually my goal when this frenzied stage of my life is over and I am free to concentrate. My daily journal continues to overflow with these new experiences both good and occasionally vaguely traumatic, but always with the view that one day I will shed this mad pace and surround myself with much-needed space. And solitude. Here I have found the space and the spiritual calm but only during the off-season when there is time to write and paint. Solitude? Never for long, there is always something happening. Words flow and I have a sense of fulfilment, that is until I read one of the authors who in my mind are gods — then I am knocked back. But only momentarily. I hope to be a writer of some depth able to impart the sensations and sentiments that I am experiencing on this ancient island. And I need to share my experiences. For me, it is always about sharing.

*

"We *must* walk the Samaria Gorge," they said as they arrived at Villa Olga.

"It's not a walk," we replied. "It's a difficult trek and can take between five to seven hours."

Some gulped and rolled their eyes in dismay; others blinked, nodded and asked further questions as we continued to explain that as yet, none of us had found the time to visit that end of the island, much less to organise a hike of the famous Samaria Gorge. We planned to of course.

"We will have to wait until we are less busy," I said, in the hope that we would always be too busy — at least until winter — but unfortunately that is not within the hiking season. I continued.

"Hikers with experience and stamina can complete the trail within three hours, but mostly it takes at least five without rushing. Wear good shoes or hiking boots, a long-sleeved shirt and a hat and go early."

A few ignored our advice and arrived back exhausted, crippled and with blisters burned by the blazing summer sun of Crete. Complaints tumbled from their cracked lips.

"There were thousands of people and all we saw were the heads of the walkers in front of us. All those tourists! Some of them refused to let us pass even though we were moving faster than they were."

"Why didn't you tell us it was such a hot and rough walk, there were rocks everywhere and rickety bridges over a fast-running stream — so dangerous! Our feet will never be the same."

We demurred politely and said we had warned them.

"Anyway, there were far too many people."

The more hardy hikers raved about the sheer beauty of the gorge, and were thrilled with the bird life, the rare wildflowers — but again the same complaint:

"There were too many people and no one spoke English! We only heard German spoken!"

Yes indeed — too many people. In high summer as many as three thousand a day make the trek down the Samaria Gorge in western Crete which is heralded as the longest gorge in Europe, and the most spectacular. The sixteen-kilometre hike is formidable and should be treated as an expedition for experienced walkers. Starting high on the Omalos Plateau the canyon cleaves its way through the region of Sfakia and the western side of the White Mountains, plunging a precipitous 1250 metres from the plateau to the Tarraios river-bed until it reaches the Libyan Sea at Ayia Roumeli. This tiny port was once the city-state of Tarrha in Greco-Roman times. The region was also the centre of Cretan independence, a wild and remote part that has remained virtually unconquered throughout the ages. The highlight of the trek is where the gorge narrows to only three metres in width known as *Sideroportes,* Iron Gates, or *Portes,* Doors. The narrow gap is less than three kilometres from Agia Roumeli.

The gorge is open from the first of May until mid-October. A multiple drowning tragedy due to flash floods has reduced the walking season until the spring rains have abated.

Recently I read of a special tour with a guide for the slow walker to take the short way up the canyon to a certain point, then return to base. It was recommended for less energetic walkers and there could still be plenty of people like me perhaps, with mobility problems or just the problem of old age, who are unable to undertake the great hike but want to experience the wonders of the gorge. It was obvious to me that one could avoid the hordes of hikers by taking the 'lazy way' with the family and no one else. We would arrive by ferry at Ayia Roumeli the little port at the base of the gorge, stay overnight and begin our uphill trek early the next morning before anyone else was awake; especially the hovering guide since we would not need one. I planned to go halfway up and then turn to head downhill back to the port; the family was unsure as to whether they would complete the uphill slog then take a bus back to eastern Crete, or turn at the halfway mark and head downhill for a swim in the gloriously refreshing waters of the Libyan Sea. Plenty to mull over when we have more time.

*

CHAPTER EIGHTEEN

GREEKS BEARING GIFTS
The washing machine

If anyone had told me I would be dissecting, cooking and eating kinds of seafood like octopus, squid and cuttlefish last year I would have given them one of my looks and totally dismissed the possibility. I have a well-documented allergy to crustaceans and a strong aversion to anything remotely *recognisable* on my plate — critters with whiskers or claws or tentacles make my stomach turn. I grew up beside the Indian Ocean with its abundance of seafood yet only ate fish per se and no shellfish of any kind though my mother loved everything from the sea. My father may have inadvertently influenced me as he suffered silently as my mother cracked her way cheerfully through crabs and various shellfish and urged him to join her,

"Come on, Jum — why don't you try one?"

Knowing full well that he would not. I suspect his system may have recognised that he too might be allergic to these same foods as I am, though the word used in those days was 'sensitive' not 'allergic'. As I was saying, for half a century I avoided all shellfish, having tried prawns once in my early twenties in Dar es Salaam when I was out having dinner with a boyfriend who urged me to try these creatures with eyes and claws that looked to me to be totally unappealing — but I acquiesced and broke out in a rash and nausea within moments — then I fainted and ended up in hospital. I can't remember what occurred there but for a warning to avoid crustaceans forever more or deal with the potentially dangerous results. At the time I was given some kind of pamphlet that described the word which I had never heard before, plus a warning to avoid these creatures in the future.

Crustacean comes from the Latin word *crusta*, which means shell. Crustaceans are a diverse collection of invertebrates such as lobsters, shrimps, crabs, krill and other names unfamiliar to me such as amphipods and copepods — I do know what barnacles look like! Since then nothing would induce me to try crustaceans again, but when the family raved and oohed and aahed at the various fish tavernas we visited, I finally agreed to try the other varieties of shellfish with my eyes tightly shut. And I was fine and enjoyed the new flavours and sensations.

Oktapothi krasato, Octopus in red wine at Aouas taverna beneath its pergola of vines turned out to be delectable, but having watched and loved the antics of these fascinating creatures underwater near The Rock I have never felt comfortable meeting them at the table. Later I grew braver and tried *kalamári,* squid, and *soupiá,* cuttlefish cooked in tomato sauce and became an instant addict. So here I am, feeling guilty and miserable because these octopuses are so intelligent; it is obvious the way they change colour and shape in an instant as they move sinuously like flowing water and turn themselves into a rock or another sea creature — almost but not quite — and the change of colour and textures is unbelievably complex as they become whatever it is into which they metamorphose. We are unable to keep up with their speed underwater but swim with our flippers as fast as we can hampered undoubtedly by our inferior intelligence. Certainly my underwater brain does not seem to work as well, or perhaps I am simply in love — in love with the octopus. I do revel when we discover them at the bottom of our rock on the sand where they can be unseen for a moment until a swirl catches the eye – and there lies a silent and still octopus, a sea creature I am sure like no other.

And back at Villa Olga there I am cutting up octopus from the market, removing the poor thing's beak and head after an initial simmering without water as it makes its own juice — and trying to pretend I am enjoying myself. Obviously I am not — and I wander about the kitchen singing quietly and wishing I had not told the family I had bought octopus for supper as I have a strong impulse to throw the lot away and give them sausages and mash. After about twenty minutes I drain off the liquid that smells rather strong and slice the now pinky-coloured octopus into small pieces and give the head and beak to the cats. I heat a cup of olive oil, sauté three sliced onions and several cloves of garlic and add the octopus which is cooked on high in a wide pan for ten minutes then I add a cup of red wine, a few chopped tomatoes, a bay leaf and simmer with a lid for two hours on *very* low heat. They tell me the sauce will thicken, it does and the dish is scrumptious served with rice and a green salad — but it is quite labour intensive and I hated cutting up the poor creature as I may well have been watching it in the iridescent sea a few days earlier. I will never again prepare this dish — but I may find it difficult to refuse it in a taverna. What does that say about me? I am a υποκριτής, ipokritís, a hypocrite; a fine Greek name and I feel ashamed at my duplicity.

I am frequently exasperated by the disparaging remarks I read in travel books on Greek food. I know mainly about Cretan food and cooking and without a doubt it is delicious. Most of the visitors who stay with us at Villa Olga return late at night after being out on the town, replete and raving about the mouth-watering flavours and the wide choice of dishes they have been introduced to, echoing my view and finally how reasonable the prices are. The food is often served warm it is true, but this is not because the stove has been switched off but because Greeks consider there is more flavour in warm food than is to be found in hot food and it is a fact. Try it and see.

*

My birthday treat from Nathalie and Julian one cold February night was a whole Λυθρίνι, lithríni, red snapper grilled over the sitting-room fire, marinated and during cooking liberally doused with olive oil, lemon juice and oregano. The spacious room filled up with aromatic smoke each time Julian poured the marinade over it and we could hardly wait to tuck into our overflowing plates. To accompany the snapper we cooked onions, courgettes and carrots in the kitchen and baked the potatoes in the ashes until they were brown and slightly burnt and split open with slabs of yellow butter salt and pepper. Oh my what a feast we had, this fish is undyingly and unforgettably delicious! For dessert Nathalie had prepared a superb fruit salad floating in red wine and thyme honey from the mountains liberally doused with cream. Delectable —καταπληκτικό — kataplitiko! Later on reflection, I realised I was a year older but age is only a number not a signal of doom and gloom I tell myself. I don't feel any older and that's what matters.

*

I have noticed that the Greeks normally do not drink unless they are eating, and when they drink they clink glasses as they toast one another with a cheery *stin yiamas* and often smack the table as well. Joyous gestures. So Greek. The sound of goblets touching is a ritual based on an ancient Greek custom that decrees all five senses should be satisfied when drinking alcohol; smell, colour, taste, touch and sound.

Plates of *mezethes,* appetisers, keep coming when one goes out for a drink in the early evening — these include cool *tzatziki* and *taramasalata,* a salty paté of cod's roe accompanied by fresh bread for dipping; slices of hard cheese called *kefalotiri* that have been dipped in water, dusted with flour then fried in hot olive oil and served with a sprinkle of lemon juice and oregano; thin crisp rounds of lightly fried μελιτζάνα, *melitzana,* eggplant and courgette; sweet herb-filled tomatoes sit on top of thick chunks of *paximathia,* rusks. The list is endless and more often than not when we dine out, our meal consists of a selection of *mezethes* plus a Greek salad. There is never room for anything else.

One of our favourite winter lunches is a hot potato salad with chunky—cut potatoes mixed with chopped onion, garlic, red and green capsicum, masses of basil and mayonnaise a little mustard and plenty of salt and pepper. The hot potatoes make the mayonnaise runny and it must be eaten hot or at least warm; once cold it tastes like any other often boring potato salad. This dish came about one cold damp afternoon when the boys came back from work starving and had forgotten to buy bread. I had nothing substantial except potatoes so I cooked up a huge pot in double quick time, mixed it with the above and it was wolfed down ravenously and pronounced the best potato salad ever. Since then it has become a favourite with my friends, easy to prepare and very filling.

A lighter, well-liked lunch is tomatoes and feta cheese sprinkled with basil on fresh brown bread bought straight from the Φούρνος, *fournos,* bakery with the green door in the square in Agios Nikolaos, or from the other along a back street in Elounda that beckons one ever inwards towards the welcoming yeasty aroma of baking bread. In Agios Nikolaos, the baker almost climbs into her huge oven still fired with olive logs to drag out the trays and we buy warm crusty loaves brown and white, for seventy drachmas each whilst exchanging pleasantries with her. She always wishes us *sto kalo,* go well, and beams behind her spectacles, her face as wrinkled as a prune. She must be well over eighty yet is up with the lark and her bakery never seems to close.

On arriving home we slice the tomatoes and feta cheese thickly, chop basil from the garden, sprinkle with salt and pepper, a dribble of olive oil and sip a glass of white wine or rosé on our balcony beneath the magenta bougainvillaea on one side and the brilliant orange Chinese trumpet flower — *bignonia grandiflora* — on the other. With the bay spread out beneath us enclosed by the Sitea mountains with the sky wide and high and bluer than blue it is almost too much, as Amanda comments. We are indeed the lucky ones. I am invariably at a loss for words to describe the drenching beauty of this place and I search for words to adequately describe how I feel without sounding trite or overly enthusiastic. But I never find them.

*

What would we do without books? One of the things that made me a bit anxious when we first came to Crete was the certain knowledge that there would be no library with English books naturally enough and that when the supply of books I had brought dried up — what would we do? My family read a lot and my life does not feel right unless I have a good book. Early on I met Mary, the Irish hairdresser who runs an informal book and magazine exchange in her upstairs salon. Friends and itinerants keep her well supplied and she has a variety of reading material from horror to science fiction to romance — but I am not into those subjects so her collection did not interest me. My reading has of necessity widened to include a few detective novels and some science fiction, but the books that have given me the most pleasure were sent to me by two friends in Australia. One is Gabriel Garcia Marquez's *Love in the Time of Cholera* that I found quite enchanting and unexpectedly humorous — so much so that I laughed aloud in the still of the night in my narrow bed, startling the visiting owl that flapped away on almost silent wings.

When we boarded the plane in Sydney last May, Julian gave me what the French reviewer calls 'The African book par excellence' bearing the proud title *The Tree where Man was Born* by Peter Matthiessen. All about East Africa my home. The author says the tree where Man was born is considered by the Nuer, a Sudanese tribe, to have stood within man's memory in south-west Sudan, and both Matthiesen — and I — believe that it was undoubtedly a great baobab, that strange tree which the natives say *Mungu*, God, turned upside-down as punishment for not growing where he wished. The outspreading tangles of branches look like roots and the wrinkled elephant-grey trunk is often thicker at the top than at the base. The bark contains calcium and is consequently 'hammered hard' by elephants Matthiesen says; nevertheless the tree lives to the great age of twenty-five hundred years and may well be the oldest living thing on earth. This book is part of my life as I lived in East Africa in all three states, mainly in Tanganyika, known as Tanzania following Independence and in Kenya and Uganda for my first twenty-eight years after which I departed with my husband and family for Australia. Matthiesen certainly knows the country and its natives well and describes them with affection and understanding.

I still miss my African home now and then especially when reading about it and sometimes wonder if we did the right thing by leaving, but politics had entered into the equation, schools were closing and it was time to seek a life elsewhere with our little family. The many years in Australia saw my children grow and become educated and gave me rewarding work in the music scene, but the overwhelming rules and regulations began to get me down. I needed to feel free somehow, to feel more satisfied with life; it was time to move to Crete. The best part of the story is that half my family decided to join me; Dame Fortune was smiling at me and continued to do so. The freedom here on this relaxed Cretan island and its friendly people are so similar in many ways that I sometimes feel as if I have gone back to East Africa; this unhurried, unharried lifestyle is comparable in so many ways

Before we left Australia Francesca gave me a classic tale called *A Thousand Miles up the Nile* by Amelia Edwards written a hundred years ago when women did not often travel up the Nile; again humorous and written with colour and flavour. Her description of a camel ride is hilarious.

Karen Blixen's *Out of Africa* has always been precious to me but it is still in Sydney with the rest of my books, cassettes and belongings while we wait to see what this season brings before having our possessions shipped. So far we have had satisfactory reservations and many summer visitors so eventually I visualise more bookshelves that we will continue to make with planks of wood painted white supported by hollow bricks lining the rough walls.

Patrick Leigh Fermor is a distinguished and scholarly writer whose books on the *Mani* of the southern Peloponnese and *Roumeli*, leave me wordless with admiration — *Roumeli* is the name once given to northern Greece — it stretches from the Bosphorus to the Adriatic and from Macedonia to the Gulf of Corinth but is not to be found on present-day maps. When I read his descriptions of the Greek world I vow once again never to touch my typewriter — for how can one succeed when masters like PLF are around? The brilliance of his writing and his sense of place and time are extraordinary and it was his book *Mani* that I discovered in Sydney before departing for Crete, that made me determined to visit that medieval and untouched region of the Peloponnese and if at all possible, to live in a Maniot watchtower and write a book.

The planting of the seed phrase comes to mind. And I *know* it will grow. It always does.

Lawrence Durrell is also one of my favourite writers. His passion for landscapes — especially Greek and Cypriot — moves something deep inside the core of me. He also writes meaningful words about those who choose to journey through their lives; he believes that journeys, similar to artists, are not made but born, no matter what they may think. Multiple different circumstances lead them to be who they are. It is their chosen path. This I do believe. Once again I realise how foolish I am to write at all. I feel inadequate and certainly in the presence of these two greats for I am so ignorant of history and in my knowledge of Greece. I feel so inept that my perennially upward curving graph line takes a slight downward turn, but only momentarily for to be sure there are many forms of writing and writers and the world is a big place with a million differing tastes. One has only to look into one of the many tourist shops in Agios Nikolaos to appreciate this where badly written paperbacks vie for shelf space with the classics and the section of Greek literature is minuscule if there at all.

With that in mind I continue to write, after all that is something I came to Crete to do as well as to sketch and paint. I have written all my life with a small amount of success in print; the need to record my thoughts has always been with me, my mind storing words and shapes and I am now doing both as though I am running out of time almost. It is a strange need that seems to have exploded since I arrived here on this island; my daily journal is overflowing with these new experiences both good and sometimes vaguely traumatic with characters met along the way, always with the view that one day I will shed my frenetic pace and surround myself with much-needed space. And solitude.

One of the books I brought with me is Durrell's *Reflections of a Marine Venus* in which he writes of those who choose to live on an island. It is a significant factor to be surrounded by sea and leads to individuality in all who have lived there for thousands of years. Cretans believe they are Cretans first and then Greeks and from what I have observed there is an innate nobility in their posture and manners that differs from other Greeks. Durrell calls them *Islomanes* — or rather Gideon does, he is one of the characters in this book who speaks for the author. To be surrounded by the sea makes the inhabitants drunk with joy, plus their compelling belief that they are the direct descendants of the inhabitants of the lost Atlantis. That they were once Atlanteans makes them special, but this according to Gideon only applies to those living on the Aegean islands.

Last but most certainly not least, Richard Bach's *Illusions* is a slim book that never leaves my bedside. If I am perplexed at life's oddities or the way things are going, I read *Illusions* and order and reason are restored in my mind. There is a pattern and for me, his philosophy is a point of reference from which all else radiates; sometimes it is necessary to withdraw from the immediate present back to that point at which all is clear. Most of Bach makes sense; it appears to be similar to Buddhist philosophy that has been mine for many years though I did not recognise it initially. I marvel at his succinct method of putting forward his views — so clear — yet in the curious form he has chosen that initially I was unable to grasp many of his concepts and had to read and re-read with my inner eye, seeking his meaning and accepting it and being comforted by it. He believes we recognise true friends as soon as we meet them because we have known them for thousands of years. This does explain to me the difference between meeting someone, whether male or female for the first time and instantly becoming close and almost bonded by their presence — and what might be called the 'normal' friendship that grows slowly over time with the sharing of ideas and values.

*

"We've found a washing machine," Julian and Jeremy announced brightly one afternoon when they returned from work, dusty and sun-tanned and about to throw themselves into the pool.

"You've *what?*"

Amanda and I shrieked, clamouring around them like children when sweets are being handed out.

"*A washing machine?*"

"Does it work?"

I asked with that slightly sinking sensation I get when things appear to be too good to be true. We had washed by hand for fourteen months and apart from the condition of my hands and nails — which also react to rubber gloves — it made my back ache intolerably. I had often wearily longed for a washing machine and in fact, had often wondered if all this was worth it. I would almost exchange it all for a washing machine, but they were horrendously expensive in Crete and we definitely could not afford one.

"Of course it works!" Julian replied scathingly.

Jeremy said, "It's an old one and they're throwing it out. We replaced it with a new one today at a farm miles away from anywhere, and they fed us with *raki*, olives, feta cheese and lots of fruit. They were so hospitable and they asked us if we wanted the old one."

Come to think of it they were both looking a bit cross-eyed; alcohol tends to have this effect on a hot afternoon. They were also looking incredibly pleased with themselves.

"If it works, then why are they throwing it out?" asked Amanda, practical and as unbelieving as myself.

"'Cause it's old!" chorused the boys.

"Because it doesn't work, more to the point," I rejoined.

"It *does* work, they told us it did. They just wanted a new one. You know the Greeks, they like to show off."

However on further questioning, it transpired that they were not absolutely sure that it *was* in working condition, but they were sure they could fix it if it wasn't. They were both handymen and loved messing around with things. Amanda gave that sort of 'aren't they sweet' smile that some women reserve especially for men and we decided to wait and see. I could not believe that our days of handwashing might finally be over. It would not be so bad if there were large hand basins or large bowls supplied, but Cretan villas do not run to these so usually it was a bucket job though for the past few months we had been doing the washing in the half-bath in Villa Two — but that still meant bending. And back-ache. I had resorted to the effective but possibly not wholesome method of washing some of my working clothes while I was still wearing them. I bought a large scrubbing brush and after a few days gardening, villa cleaning and sweeping I would step into the shower — heated by solar heating and always hot — and scrub my clothes with the brush and soap. It worked very well and I also had a stimulating body massage to boot. Then I took them off and rinsed them.

Nikos the electrician in Agios Nikolaos, the plump, smiling Cretan with fair hair and light eyes who was afraid of heights, asked

Julian and Jeremy if they minded working on rooftops and in high places. They said they didn't mind. I wondered how Nikos managed, perhaps he only worked at ground level?

"Bravo!" he said.

"You will make the work in high places because I am afraid for them."

So while Julian and Jeremy did the work in the high places, Nikos held the ladder with his eyes averted moaning with exaggerated fear as the boys fooled around on the roof, pretending to fall or go dizzy and stumble down the ladder, giving Nikos minor heart attacks. They installed everything from water pumps in mountain villages in ancient wells and fridges in hamlets of three or four cottages hidden in deep valleys to strobe lighting in the latest disco bars and hotels — and occasionally exchanged old washing machines for new.

Amazing! We were to have a washing machine I mused as I woke the following day, wondering where we would put it. It was the height of the summer season and we were all currently living in the largest Villa Two, having moved in as the reservations piled up. There was no room in the bathroom with its non-functioning bidet — some flight of fantasy in Mikalis' fertile imagination — a bidet — *in Crete*? The kitchen was not spacious enough — the washing machine would have to go outside. In the courtyard off the kitchen.

"*Outside*?" they all exclaimed.

"Where else? There's nowhere except the front veranda."
An inspection was made. Yes, it would have to go into the courtyard shaded by the apricot tree. A nice touch I thought. The great day came. Nikos loaned them his truck; they could hardly bring it on their scooters and with help from several of our guests, the washing machine was hauled up the terraces up the steps to the veranda and through the house into the courtyard. It looked enormous. It *was* enormous. Ugly too. I did not like it.

Before doing anything further we collapsed around the pool; cold drinks all round and swam to refresh ourselves before tackling the monster in the courtyard. First we had to translate the Greek instructions which was difficult as there were so many cycles; ten I believe; all illustrated with little drawings that we could not fully

240

understand. It worried me. I have a distrust of anything that is not simple; stoves, fridges, watches and washing machines. For me 'on — wash — rinse-off' is sufficient. I did not want to know the rest, just that it worked when I switched on the knob. The boys fixed various lengths of hose and electric cables to the machine and inside to the taps and power points, leading them out of the kitchen door into the courtyard until it resembled someone on a life support system. We squatted around the glass side-opening door and watched with bated breath when Julian switched it on — having saved our dirtiest clothes for this christening. Nothing. Then strange sounds — a gurgling and a bubbling — air moving around. Suddenly we saw water coming in very slowly, but it *was* filling up. Whoops of triumph and visions of all the washing we had been saving up coming out pristine clean and shining. No more backache — well not so many. Soft smooth hands like the awful television advertisements. Truly a day for a celebration. Well — it filled up then sat silent and brooding while we waited in suspense for something to happen. Nothing did.

"Perhaps it's heating up?" Someone said encouragingly.

"But we haven't got it on the hot cycle!"

Hopes dashed. We clicked it round one notch onto another cycle and it groaned and moaned and began to spin the water out onto the orange tree at the side of the villa, heaving and sighing as it emptied itself. It was *very* noisy.

"Well — at least it empties OK," someone said encouragingly.

"But it didn't do a wash cycle did it?" I said sarcastically and received such dirty looks that I removed myself and prepared supper while the boys hummed and muttered and pulled things apart. Amanda and Jenny took themselves off on the scooters to town to perform their musical gigs and I pretended there wasn't a washing machine lurking in the courtyard.

When Julian decides to fix a thing he fixes it come hell or high water but by midnight he and Jeremy gave up and left it in bits all over the courtyard. My heart sank. Loads of washing couldn't wait till the weekend when they decided to tackle it again, but did it matter? No, not really. I chose to forget about the dirty clothes and take myself off to The Rock for a swim and some meditation. Why do we not do this more often I asked myself — we have this in-built sense of duty and work ethic instilled into us and it is hard to put aside. But I am doing well, after all tomorrow is another day in this paradise.

Eventually after many false starts and taking apart and experiments we found two cycles that worked, but the short one took three hours and sometimes inexplicably, even longer and there seemed to be nothing we could do about it.

"At least it's washing *and* rinsing," remarked Julian one day from his favourite position, squatting by the machine and gazing intently on it as it chugged — or didn't chug — onto the next cycle. It had taken three hours and was still going around and stopping, thinking about things unwilling to shift into the final emptying phase.

"Even if it does take half a day," I added and got a squirt of water from the hose from my son.

We became inured to the time factor and told ourselves we were grateful for small mercies though we did wonder about the electricity bill that was going to soar. Our clothes lost stains that we had told ourselves were there for good and a pair of dark tan shorts of mine came out a creamy coffee shade that I had completely forgotten over the months I had been wearing them. It was a godsend but for the dreadful noise that the monster machine made. It emitted a variety of sounds, a moaning and grunting before it spun and then a high-pitched squeaking that grew in intensity to an ear-splitting banshee wail which could be heard from the road below the boys told us.

They decided once more — and definitely for the last time — to take it apart. But it was never the same after that and the noise was so loud we could not use it when there were people in the villas above ours, it was just too intrusive. I began to hate it more and more and longed for the tranquillity of the quiet old days of hand-washing.

*

It lasted about five months becoming progressively more reluctant and argumentative not to mention slower and slower until the *short* cycle took six hours. When Mikalis produced the electricity bill it was so high we all took to drink in a big way and our love affair with the washing machine was decidedly over. Yiannis came with his big truck and they took it away to the dump which was where it should have gone in the first place. We gave a sigh of relief and returned to our old lifestyle, even our dinner conversation reverted back to normal. Instead of,

"How long did it take today?" and

"You mean it actually did the *whole* cycle in three and a half hours? Impressive!" We discussed the *meltemi* and the failure of the ferry and the planes to arrive with our clients; whether we should go to a favoured spot in town for some fish or pop over the brow of the hill for a glass of *rosé* and fresh fruit at the little taverna in Ellinika. Oh what choices —are we not the lucky ones?

*

Magic in music enters one's life at the most unlikely times. I had been looking at some land with a new acquaintance who was thinking of moving to Crete; it was late afternoon the rain had set in and we were both hungry.

"Do you like fish?" he asked.

"Absolutely," I replied.

We drove to a little taverna right on the seafront at Pacheia Ammos and sat by a large window looking out onto the foaming sea. It was a wild stormy day, quite cold with wonderful angry seas and skies full of sulky clouds and shafts of sunlight. And rainbows. Above the dark skyline, a double rainbow — two perfect curves of colour and I made my wish — I do not know what he wished for.

We chose the most delectable *bourbouni,* red mullet with hot bread and village wine and watched the light fade from the wild sky beyond the window; warm inside, plastic on the tables the senses intoxicated by the tones of a Cretan lyre from a crackly radio, lively Greek voices and laughter, the aroma of herbs, fresh bread, village wine and finally the thick sweetness of Greek coffee.

"It could only be Crete," we agreed.

Outside — through windows misty and rain-streaked tamarisk trees tossed and twisted held captive by the capricious wind. Then we saw a bearded man, thick-set with a ponytail at the far end of the long dark jetty in the teeth of the wind, seemingly oblivious to the waves crashing against the sides, loose trousers and jacket flapping. He began to dance — Cretan style with arms outstretched fingers clicking and knees together — bending and swaying from side to side. He turned to face the shore, throwing his arms into the air as he looked up towards the mountains as if in supplication to the elements then confronted the churning sea and made the same expansive gesture. One of gratitude. A man in love with the world around him with the lyre's haunting notes in his brain. It was so moving my friend took my hand in his and we watched in silence. Spellbound.

The dancing man reminded me of Zorba who when everything had blown away and he had nothing left, danced alone. Only the dancing helped his pain. I wondered if the man was in pain and I was sure he must be Cretan. I was equally sure he was dancing to the same music we were hearing in the warmth of the taverna, but when he came through the door I saw he was middle-aged with deep-set blue eyes and had a Walkman on his chest.

He greeted a companion sitting at one of the tables, speaking in German. This was no Greek but a man who felt — and danced — like one.

*

CHAPTER NINETEEN

A CHOIR OF THREE THOUSAND VOICES
The Verdi Requiem in Verona

Italy! I am on my first visit and the goal? To sing the *Verdi Requiem* in the World Festival Choir of three thousand voices with Luciano Pavarotti and conductor Lorin Maazel. And the venue? The Arena di Verona, that ancient amphitheatre the centre of summer festivals since Roman times. And I am going to be a part of it. The World Festival Choir will perform on the fourth and fifth of August 1990.

*

The land approaching Venice is flooded for miles. The inhabitants of the Byzantine *Duchy of Tre Venezie* attempting to escape the barbarians built the city on marshland. Approaching by air is spectacular with so much water and seemingly so little land. Luckily there are helpful people at the airport and the bus station since I am travelling on my own in a foreign country without speaking the language, and although I love the idea I must admit to feeling collywobbles in the pit of my stomach, or is it just excitement? Tall buildings; steeply pitched roofs with red tiles and narrow arched windows; overhanging balconies; walls glowing warm mustard and apricot stucco with coffee and greeny-blue trim; turquoise arches — wonderful Italian colour combinations — and gardens with spreading green trees, chestnuts, magnolia bushes standing in bright verdant grass all glimpsed from the window of the bus that takes me slowly from the airport to Padova, Padua. The land is so fertile and lush after Crete — restful to my eyes and my soul. I need a change from summer harshness. It is evening in late July and my almost empty bus is about to deposit me at the Sheraton Hotel, thirty-seven kilometres from Venice.

The terrain changes and becomes flat and densely cultivated with field after field of maize for this is rich land agriculturally; the chequered landscape is bordered by tree and shrubs pleasing to look at. Soft. A house of many storeys with round windows above curved ones — all the buildings are many-storied and narrow — they stand between trellised grapes, very green. Willows lean over a river. This really *feels* like Italy and I am so thrilled to see different styles of architecture after the simple Aegean lines of Crete, and here there are no ugly concrete unfinished skeletons of houses to mar the skyline. I sense pride and dignity in this Italian land often sadly missing in Greece.

Now I am in the modern and characterless Sheraton Hotel outside Padova and meet up with other choristers who are arriving by the busload. I discover it is a very long way outside the town and this becomes a problem since even a cup of coffee is so hideously expensive that none of us can afford to eat or drink at the hotel, and it's too far to walk to the town. Luckily there is a little store nearby where we find the necessities of life. The hotel is also quite a distance from the bus stop. Inconvenient. The large Australian contingency of choristers had no choice of where they stayed — they merely paid the bills. Some of the more fortunate were put in a country-style hotel with beautiful grounds, pool, health spas and paid a lot less than we did. I never did discover what lottery landed us in the Sheraton. My Sydney friend Pat has not arrived yet — at least that is what they tell me. Strange — she said she would be here yesterday. They are somewhat flustered at the desk and I suspect there is probably a message for me somewhere. I have poured a gin and tonic from the fridge mainly to try to appease the knife-sharp pain down my sciatic nerve that is giving me hell — my bag was far too heavy for me. Carrying weights these last few years has had an immediate and damaging effect on my grafted spine and the sciatic nerve gets trapped.

What am I to do I agonise sipping my gin and tonic. How can I be independent when I am unable to carry the necessities of life without ending up in debilitating pain? I feel extremely tired and a bit depressed yet I started from Crete feeling elated and excited, I am now writing postcards in the unfriendly room and wonder why is it that everyone I know feels the need to write postcards on arrival in a new place — must be a sign of deep-seated insecurity I suppose. It is pretty pointless as I will be back in Crete in ten days but it forms a link with the familiar and is comforting. So here am I — writing pointless postcards, drinking gin which is improving my mood if not my pain, when in walks Pat. She *had* left a message to say she was out for the day in a hire car and when she asked at the desk if I had arrived, they said no. The hotel is poorly managed.

It got worse! That same evening Amanda, my daughter who had arrived in Padova the night before, had rung twice to see if I was there and no one knew anything about me. I felt almost as if I did not exist. Eventually she and Jeremy caught up with me and we spent a few wonderful hours together before parting once more. They had said goodbye to me and to Crete months ago and headed for London where Jeremy found himself a fantastic position as *sous chef* in a Holland Park restaurant, a stylish part of London. Amanda also was working with the Californian Wine Institute. What an elegant, willowy creature my middle daughter has become; I always forget how beautiful she is and am so delighted when I see her again. Her hugs are strong but spindly, her long arms seem to go around me more than once and I feel very safe when I am near her. I tell her it is a bit like being hugged by a beautiful grasshopper.

Finally Patricia and I are reunited after a year; we last met in Sydney before I took off on my Cretan adventure. Who would have thought we would meet up in a hotel room in Padova, singing together and sharing such a fantastic experience? We are overjoyed and despite the gruelling rehearsal schedule we manage to celebrate and relax — often until well after midnight — as we sit on our beds and sustain our flagging spirits with a nightcap of heady *grappa*-drenched purple plums, snacks of cheese and crusty bread. We are having the best time of our lives.

The journey by coach to the enchanting walled city of Verona and the ancient arena each time we rehearse takes an hour and a half; sometimes it is in the mornings; sometimes mid-afternoon when the temperature reaches forty degrees and people faint and we have had two rehearsals starting at eleven p.m. because the stage was continuously in use by the other productions, so rehearsal time was tight. On those occasions we got back to the hotel at three in the morning quite worn out; even so we made time for our night-cap and it did help.

The Moscow Philharmonic Orchestra players are also suffering from the heat. The all-male musicians wear hankies on their heads and look like the British on holiday at Blackpool — not that I have ever been there — and the basses have small umbrellas over their instruments. Today the temperature was forty-five degrees and Lorin Maazel, our conductor who has finally arrived only two days before the first performance, has sent us home. It was too hot. He gave us a right royal bollocking and told us he despaired of the performance ever getting off the ground; that we were *not* concentrating and that we were *not* good enough and so on. I wonder what Jan Jensen thinks; he is the artistic and managing director of the World Festival Choir and has been our conductor since day one. However I do know from my experience in the opera house in Sydney, that conductors use all sorts of wiles to get the best out of their choirs and musicians and more often than not, throw a tantrum just before opening night.

The idea of a requiem mass sung by a choir from all nations goes back a long way. Five years in fact, and was co-ordinated by Jensen and Bjorn Simensen director of the Norske Opera in Norway. They organised twenty-five rehearsal centres throughout the world with as many choir-masters and pianists, and rehearsals of the Verdi Requiem commenced with special instructions on performance from Lorin Maazel. I had been a member of the Sydney Philharmonia Choir and had sung the requiem several times so when Pat wrote and told me of the event in Verona, I felt I simply *had* to be a part of it. I wrote to the powers-that-be and asked if I could join them having sung the requiem in Sydney and that I still had my score. To my delight and surprise they said yes, so with cassette and my score with the new conductor's markings, I practised my second alto part outside in the garden when there were no clients around – much to the amusement of Mikalis as he fussed nearby on the terrace. And dreamed of Verona. And finally here I was.

*

Pat and I managed several trips to Venice that was so much smaller than I imagined it would be. It was a world on its own, to me not part of the twentieth century at all; the delicate architecture of arches and scrolls and tracery lending an air of enchantment to the skyline. I loved the watery city from the moment we chugged into the canals on the *vaporetti,* water buses; despite the heat and the crowds the magic seeped in and I told Pat I intended to return out of season with a lover and stay in an apartment over one of the back canals. What a dream. But my dreams have a way of coming true. I am living in Crete am I not, and was that not my dream many years before I finally got there?

Venice was cleaner than I had been led to expect and less noxious — only once did we come across a nasty smell and after experiencing Cretan summer drains it was positively pleasant. The gondolas are larger and longer than I imagined they would be, black by decree and so graceful, like tethered swans they rock gently back and forth in unison as the gondoliers bend over a single 'rowlock' or 'oarlock' on the right side with a long oar. They probably have over-developed muscles in their backs and shoulders and to me look as if they have come straight out of a musical with their white shirts, black pants, straw hats and ribbons. And they do sing! Interestingly my knowledgeable friend Pat tells me that the waters of Venice are too deep for the gondolas to be poled like a punt, contrary to popular belief.

The Doge's Palace reminds me of a pink birthday cake with its delicate filigree work and double arches and the pink and white mosaics that cover the external walls give the place an air of femininity, also an eastern feel about its shape — hardly European. Lovely. Pat and I toured a marvellous exhibition of Titian's works and miniature glassware in the palace and I bought my daughters some earrings. The shops in the winding streets are quite superb — each tiny window a work of art — like a studio set for a photograph, quite unreal awfully expensive and a bit daunting. One got the impression that without a twin-set and pearls or a mink coat one would not be welcome within their sacred portals so we kept out.

Italians are a most attractive race with their soft lilting voices and language, there is music in everything they say and physically they are so beautiful with their perfect skins, dark eyes and masses of curling glossy hair. And their fashion sense — the cut of their silk shirts and blouses — the sheen of good leather shoes and handbags — stunning. They are blessed with a natural elegance and a gift with fabric and design that the world recognises of course, but that I had not previously seen. What is more, they appear to be happy and contented people with a ready laugh, beautiful teeth in those smooth olive faces framed in their dark locks. They are a race most welcome at Villa Olga and almost my favourite guests.

The only fly in the ointment in the hotel was the ever-present anxiety about theft. We were constantly warned to be careful not to leave things unguarded that I found so difficult after the relaxed Cretan honesty where theft is virtually unknown. There were two cases of theft amongst our choir members who were left without money, passports and papers and were seriously distressed, and the desk — as if it were not disorganised already — was not allowed to keep large amounts of cash for traveller's cheques owing to gangs with machine-guns that reputedly held up hotels known to carry significant sums of money. We had to return again and again to await the next arrival of the armoured van before we could get our cheques cashed.

*

One night the entire choir and orchestra were invited to a famous Palladian villa some distance from Padova. Coach-load after coach-load disgorged we choristers and musicians in our glad rags and we wandered around the vast buildings and into a villa where every inch of wall was covered in decorations of rather disturbing colours.
 "Couldn't live with *this* could you Pat?"
I muttered as we went into the first room and then the next and then the next, even the outer walls were covered with gaudy paintings. After a long wait, we were fed beneath huge marquees by hundreds of chefs carving hunks of ham and roast pork on trestle tables and we helped ourselves to salads and rolls and wine. Then some dignitary or other gave a speech followed by another and another — all rather boring and we were tired and suffering from the intense heat in the

crowded space milling with people. The temperature did not seem to go down in the evenings, the heat hung around with no respite at the end of the day and we both craved a cool bath, some light sustenance and a night of long sleep. We could have done without the bad management of both hotel and the people in charge of the travel arrangements for the choir; we often had to stand around for hours for the coaches to arrive, then wait again in the buses that for one reason or another were held up; sometimes they did not come at all, often they lost groups of choristers who had to find their own way back from Verona to Padova. There was no one to whom we could go with a query and be sure of a satisfactory answer; totally inept they were and Pat and I vowed never again to join a World Festival Choir event. I accept that the task of looking after three thousand people of thirty different nationalities was enormous, yet the actual seating and rehearsals and musical content was well organised, I could not fault it. We each had coloured tickets with numbers that gave us entry and exit through only one door and led us to our seats around the amphitheatre, and our entrances and exits were quiet, orderly and fast.

*

On the night seated high in the two-thousand-year-old Arena di Verona feeling the sun's heat through the old stones and around me the sky-line of churches, spires and belfries silhouetted against the full moon rising pale and the red sun going down in a spectacular sunset, though some cynic told me that pollution was responsible for the blazing sunsets each evening. Below, the sound of horses' hooves on the cobbled streets, church bells chiming the hours and the knowledge that people have sat in this same place for thousands of years, made this one of the most exciting moments of my life. We were spread over the dumpy steps of the amphitheatre in the shape of a stylised dove, its white 'wings' formed by the white blouses of the sopranos and altos while the central 'body' was formed by the black shirts of the male choristers. The performance was linked to the forty-fifth anniversary of the dropping of the bomb on Hiroshima and the singers from Japan, some of whom had lost their entire families on that dreadful day in August, outnumbered us.

As the ranks of celli with mutes produced the descending notes that mysteriously opened the Requiem Mass tears flooded into my eyes and I could not see my score. I looked around — the moment was almost too much to bear. We were all crying as we whispered with our three thousand voices *sotto voce il piu piano possible,* which translates as *"*under the voice as softly as possible"

"Requiem — *Requiem-ae-ter-nam* Rest and peace. Rest and peace et-er-nal."

And as we sang the twenty-five thousand spectators lit candles and tiny points of light appeared around the arena and I came out in goose bumps. The atmosphere was electric; nothing moved but the conductor's arms and the bows of the string players far below on the stage. It was as if the world had stopped breathing.

And Pavarotti. When the orchestra and choir and soloists were in full flight I could hear his mighty voice soaring above ours — it was sensational. During rehearsal he limped badly and was in obvious pain — gout? He wore a Hawaiian shirt and a huge towel around his shoulders and resembled an unmade bed and was not in full voice — but then all soloists preserve their voices during rehearsal. But the elegantly dressed dignity of the performing Pavarotti was a different picture. There were banners outside the Arena reading 'Luciano you are great!' and the thunderous roar when he made his entrance confirmed his popularity — and his performance earned it. The other soloists — Sharon Sweet, Dolora Zajick and Paul Plishka — were, in comparison not as strong, but the ensuing rave reviews in the local newspapers pronounced them as fitting co-singers with the great Pavarotti.

And as we murmured the epilogue of the *Libera Me*, Save me, Oh Lord, Save me, Oh Lord — written *pppp morendo* in our scores — and our voices died away I thought I would burst with emotion and pride. Following the final *Sanctus* the audience stayed quiet for a few moments — too moved to make a sound. Reluctant to break the spell. Then the applause broke out and everyone went *wild* and I saw for the first time, crowd hysteria of the best kind, crowd hysteria as only the Italians know how. Hats and pillows were thrown into the air and people stood on each other's shoulders and shrieked and clapped and whistled. The applause went on for twenty minutes with Maazel and the soloists walking to and from the side of the stage and the choir standing and sitting down on command until we were all totally exhausted. Wrung out.

And the next night the same again with an equally ecstatic crowd; a whisper ran around the choir, Princess Diana was in the audience. Dame Fortune smiled on our performances and us because the following night we went en masse to see 'Aida' and it rained! I watched with amusement as several little men with huge bundles of plastic raincoats fought their way through the tiers of people in the audience trying to sell their coats at twice the price they had been before the concert. But raincoats did not help. The performance was washed out and we went home extremely disappointed. And the next day we all flew away.

CHAPTER TWENTY

THIS SEA-BEATEN HOME OF OURS
Jazz to the island?

At last the summer is abating and there is a hint of autumn in the air. The strident cicadas no longer puncture the afternoon's silence with their harsh chords, the ubiquitous prickly pear or Frankish fig as the Cretans call this spiny cactus, is smothered with round yellow fruit and the pomegranates are ripe to bursting and very sweet. The wasps are delighted. This welcome and blessed relief from the heat came with two days of solid rain, hard big drops that flooded the balcony of the villa as the drain on the flat roof emptied itself beside the front door of the villa below; why would anyone have a drain pipe beside a front door I ask myself? Not only did it flood into our villa but also it dripped into the tiny narrow kitchen space in Villa One immediately beneath us, much to the consternation of the young couple staying there.

Mikalis arrived following my urgent telephone call and drew his black brows together then looked skywards at the leaden clouds and said wisely, *"Provlema."* Talk about stating the obvious.

"Nai!" I said. Then in uncertain Greek, "We have a problem, but what are you going to do about the problem?"

The tiles on the balcony were separating and would need replacing he growled and stomped away in a dark rage. Predictably, nothing was done. A few days later when Julian and I stated the need for immediate action before the next visitors arrived — fortunately we were able to move the young couple into another villa. Mikalis frowned again and said,

"Isos." Perhaps he could get the tiler next week *"Isos,"* he said again as he charged off down the terraces to his car.

"Probably never see him again," remarked Julian humorously. He has become so Greek in his acceptance of the status quo — there is no point in becoming agitated or frustrated in Greece, it just does not work.

The garden is lifting its head after the blazing heat and the many hundreds of brown and gold marigolds that only just survived from one watering to another and did not bloom, are now in full glory and the air is filled with their pungent scent. The roses are in bloom once again and the rather sulky bougainvillaea under the pool and the other by our villa steps, have both perked up and there are sprays of purple and magenta flowers. A celebration of colour. It is also cool enough to write again if I can find the time. I found it increasingly difficult to concentrate on creative things during the summer and this disturbed me profoundly as I had not come to Crete to find myself as busy as I was in Australia; but it has also been an unusually torrid and over-crowded summer, the Cretans assure me, they too have suffered and the phrase πολύ ζεστό, poli zesto, very hot, was at the forefront of every greeting. The intense pleasure we are all experiencing as we can once more sit on the balcony in the early morning without being scorched is heartfelt; we are all worn out after nearly six months of unrelenting heat. I began to think if I had to drive Buttercup into town once more to shop, collect and deliver linen, stock up our little shop, exchange gas cylinders and collect the mail once more I would expire — but of course I didn't — but I was becoming bone-weary and also extremely tired of being at the beck and call of all the summer visitors, twenty-four hours a day.

A factor that most certainly led to our combined exhaustion was the time of arrival and departure of the flights from the UK as they arrived when the airport landing fees were at their lowest, i.e. between midnight and dawn. This meant that our outgoing visitors stayed on until around ten or eleven at night since I never had the heart to turf people out at midday as is the custom, and following their departure we had to clean the villas thoroughly, replace the dirty linen in preparation for the new arrivals from overseas who had disembarked on the same plane that would carry their predecessors back to their homes. The only compensation for these mid-nightly cleanings was that it was the coolest part of the day. We had devised a system whereby the newcomers knew which villa they would be occupying beforehand, the garden lights were programmed to come on before their time of arrival so they could let themselves in without disturbing us — but it didn't always happen that way.

Our villas were self-catering and we supplied a free welcome basket containing a bottle of Cretan wine and all the necessities for a good breakfast including fresh fruit so that the need to go shopping could be delayed until they had a rest, so we thought of everything. Nonetheless, more often than not we would be wakened by a knock on the door having only got to bed possibly an hour before, by someone asking an idiotic question the answer to which — had they read the information sheet provided — was spelt out. My agents in Australia and the UK also sent out information sheets with our classy black and white three-fold brochure describing succinctly what to expect in a traditional Cretan-style villa. I was continually amazed to find that so many of our clients arrived with little or no knowledge of what to expect, despite our efforts to apprise them of the idiosyncrasies of this culture beforehand.

*

Looking back over the past eighteen months since our arrival I am forced to admit I have failed in several schemes I felt sure I could achieve. I wanted to bring an orchestra to Crete to perform in the summer festivals that continue for weeks both in Agios Nikolaos and Heraklion. On my arrival, I met the mayor of Agios Nikolaos who had once studied the violin, and when I told him of my plan he put his head to one side and said in a tired voice,

"It is a wonderful idea Valerie, but we are very poor. This town has no money."

I scoffed politely and said I would have thought that Agios Nikolaos would have been the wealthiest town in Crete. He agreed that it *should* be the wealthiest then added,

"But no one pays any taxes you know. No one pays any taxes." This we had already discovered. The Cretans — and I expect this applies to most Greeks — are experts at devising schemes to evade the payment of taxes. It is the subject of many a long dissertation over cups of coffee or miniature glasses of ouzo or raki. The mayor sent me to Heraklion and invited me to dinner at the same time so Julian and I went to the mayor with our plan, but there was no money there either. Two weeks later our mayor phoned to remind me of his dinner invitation and would my daughter like to come too.

We certainly would I assured him and a few days later Francesca and I joined him for dinner at the Gargadoros Fish Taverna overlooking the sparkling bay on one side and an early cemetery on the other. Our host was treated like royalty, with great respect and obvious fondness by everyone around us and a bearded Cretan at a table nearby, insisted on buying the red wine for us and we drank one another's health throughout the evening. I did notice the mayor paid for the meal when we left, rejecting the earnest pleas of the offer of a free evening from the patron. He is a refined and mannerly gentleman of the old school who regaled us with his exploits during the German occupation when he was one of the leaders of the Resistance. He was arrested several times and under sentence in prison but managed to escape on both occasions. He revealed that he was tired of being mayor and was looking forward to his retirement at the end of the year. Amusingly, after our delicious meal of crispy *marithes* piled high on the large plates with golden chips and a crisp and inviting Greek salad, he asked for two 'doggy-bags' — one for his cats and one for ours. A nice homely man.

*

Next project. Knowing how much the Cretans love jazz, Julian and I attempted to introduce British jazz to eastern Crete; we approached several large hotels and nightclubs with proposals that met with a great deal of interest. Through my English composer friend Tim Souster, we had contacts in Britain and bands ready and willing to play on the island. We impressed the sons of the hotel owners with our budgets and plans but when it came to trying to persuade their elderly fathers, mainly uneducated men of great wealth and no imagination — suspicious too — we came up against a brick wall. Their sons could see the kudos in being the only place to have live British jazz and could imagine what a financial success it could be, but not their fathers. They were making a fortune without expending any extra energy so why bother? It was disappointing initially as we felt the need for another string to our bow; the villas were bringing in little income; we were paying Mikalis far too much for the pleasure of leasing them and my small capital was dwindling fast. Julian's had gone down the drain and something had to be done.

There was no live music in Agios Nikolaos or Elounda apart from that provided by Amanda and Jenny who played at several of the large hotels; the only other music was the occasional Cretan or Greek night that was geared solely for tourists at which no local would be seen dead. Most of the visitors at Villa Olga found this organised entertainment embarrassing in the extreme as they were encouraged to join the Cretan dancers with other tourists — not from Villa Olga, I hasten to add — who were often extremely drunk, falling over and behaving in a disorderly and embarrassing fashion. There seemed to be no entertainment for the discerning visitor. Jazz would have been ideal and according to the Cretans, British jazz was the best. Their disappointment was profound when we finally explained the entire concept was proving to be too difficult, too complicated to fulfil, not to mention their fathers' refusals to even consider the idea.

*

Later and with hindsight, we realised it would have been an absolute nightmare to organise. We had traced the only double bass on the island which was in Heraklion and in doubtful condition, drum kits were available as was a piano, but our contacts seemed to be incredulous — they simply rolled their eyes — "A piano tuner?" they echoed in Greek of course. My vocabulary was advancing by the day. I began to realise that our escape from stress which was part of the reason for coming to Crete in the first place, would have been negated so I was mightily relieved when the whole plan fell through. I am not sure how Julian felt but we agreed we might try again next year and to feed the longing I have to listen to the classics and opera I make do with cassettes — it's a lot easier.

*

The longer I live the more I appreciate Greek philosophy and am continually impressed by their highly developed thought processes, quite unlike that of any other culture I have come across, not that I am an expert on this subject. This must appear to be a sweeping statement but ask a Greek or a Cretan a question of some profundity and after a short pause you will get an answer that will probably surprise you by its depth of understanding. My ex-teacher Dimitris, a quiet, bespectacled man with a droll sense of humour had returned to Crete from Canada but refused point-blank to give me any lessons as he was too busy, having taken up the unenviable position of managing Kalithea — a complex of new villas around a swimming pool, overlooking the gap between Agios Nikolaos and Elounda — a mere stone's throw from our villas.

One quiet evening over a drink at the bar as the copper sky turned the waters of the bay to fire, I asked him what it was that made Greeks arrive at such intuitive and interesting conclusions. Was it that they came from the long line of some of the world's greatest thinkers and philosophers or was it something else?

Dimitris sipped his glass of red thoughtfully then said,

"Partly, and we Greeks have not lost the art of discourse and argument. We, like you get our news through the media but with you that is where it often stops. It is accepted as fact — or maybe fiction — and not necessarily discussed at length during that day. With us Greeks it is different. We sit in the *kafenion* or outside our villas and we argue about everything we have heard for hours. Every day this happens. We always find time to do this because it is important to us. We speak with all kinds of people; shepherds, shopkeepers, waiters, farmers, politicians; they all have their opinion of what they have heard and we exchange points of view. Sometimes with much heat as you would know!" And he grinned.

"This is how we look at a subject — from many sides. It is a daily need for a Greek to confer with his fellowmen."

I thought he had put it in a nutshell. We in the western world have become too busy, too preoccupied with making money or seeking success of some kind which more often than not brings us no peace of mind, merely more stress and responsibility. One of the things I noticed when we first arrived was how rewarding it was to have the time for discourse and a prolonged cup of coffee and I vowed I would never exchange this way of life for my old routine, whether or not I remained in Greece I would endeavour to leave time for friends, family and relaxation in the future. And for now I need to be able to confer in Greek, it is my greatest desire. I want to master this rich and descriptive language and wander into the more remote villages in the mountains and speak or more importantly listen to the old people and the shepherds, those pale-eyed aristocrats of the high places who greet me with a certain cautious interest and with whom I have a fierce desire to communicate; they have such stories to tell and they live to a great age on this island. Even in the little hamlet of Ellinika above our villas, those wise-looking *yia-yias* in black chatter to me like magpies, not realising that I am only able to understand half of what they are saying and that I am pathetically incompetent at expressing myself. I nod, smile and reply. *"Nai, nai,"* Yes, yes, in agreement and wish I were as fluent as they appear to think I am. I shall be one day. More study is called for. I love the language but the lack of time to study is eluding me now. Find it, Valerie — find the time!

*

After living here for a while we have established a few favourite haunts where we are greeted like old friends and offered a glass of raki and a small plate of *mezethes* while we decide what to order. If that is not a sufficient example of a delightful Cretan tradition — having eaten to our heart's content and preparing to leave with a warm *kalinychta*, kalinikta, goodnight — we are urged to stay and offered a selection of fruit in season to round off the evening. Generosity personified, how fortunate are we?

*

Sweet night — dark as velvet — warm air soft as melted chocolate. The breeze touches my skin as I relax on a chaise longue by the silent pool. Apart from the cats that have followed me onto the terrace everyone is asleep, or possibly some of the residents are still out carousing in one of the nightclubs in twinkling Agios Nikolaos far below. It is quiet and so restful after the hectic pace of the day and I am content as I reflect on the occasional visitors, male or female with whom I have established a spark of real friendship; they will stay for a week or a fortnight, seldom longer, then fly off into the night as I prepare their villas for the next incumbent. When they depart, I am happy to remain here at Villa Olga and I believe I always will be, though I do have a fleeting sense of loss which is reflected in Henry Wadsworth Longfellow's sensitive poem from his book of poems based on real people:

Tales of a Wayside Inn

Ships that pass in the night, and speak each other in passing,
Only a signal shown and a distant voice in the darkness;
So on the ocean of life, we pass and speak one another,
Only a look and a voice, then darkness again and a silence.

*

Goethe considered the Greeks above all people, had dreamt the dream of life best and I believe he got it right. I for one intend to remain on this sea-beaten island for it is the fulfilment of my long dream and I do not have another. My family will come and go. Friends old and new will come and go glorying in the charm of the Cretan people, the island's light and the blue of sea and sky but for now I am staying here.

to telos

Author's note: All the information given in this book was accurate at the time of writing, but may not be so on the date of publication.

Villa Olga

Villa Olga

Villa Olga

Ellinika

- ❏ *Exclusive holiday villas*

- ❏ *Located 7km north of Agios Nikolaos on Elounda bus route*

- ❏ *Villas are self contained, airy and comfortable*

- ❏ *Furnished in traditional Cretan style*

- ❏ *Solar/electric heating*

- ❏ *Each has balcony or courtyard*

- ❏ *Panoramic views*

- ❏ *In ground swimming pool*

- ❏ *Small shop located within the Villa grounds*

- ❏ *Open 12 months of the year*

- ❏ *Negotiable rates for group bookings (archaeological, photographic, artists, clubs etc)*

- ❏ *Run by English/Australian family*

Villa Olga

Ellinika
Crete

Six individual studios and villas, set in exotic gardens overlooking Mirambellou Bay.